ADVANCE PRAISE FOR OFF CENTER

"If there's someone you love struggling with addiction, *Off Center* is a must-read. Randy takes you behind the scenes to the dark side of being a professional athlete, through the trenches of addiction, and shows how chronic pain is so often the gateway to the hell of prescription drug addiction, regardless of your profession. Weaving in his own personal struggles with addiction and path to recovery, Randy also shares an intimate look into the process of an intervention and the rewards of recovery. I see why Randy is one of the most sought-after interventionists. Fast-paced while filled with warmth, humility, and candor, *Off Center* delivers hope for anyone struggling with addiction and everyone who loves them."

—Michael Sprintz, DO, DFASAM, (triple-board certified) chronic pain and addiction expert with twenty-plus years of personal recovery

"I saw something very special in Randy Grimes, while recruiting him from high school to Baylor University. I saw a leader, a warrior, someone who would battle through any obstacle to reach his goals. The pages of this book just reaffirm what I already knew. Nothing, not even addiction, could ever keep Randy Grimes down. A great comeback story!"

—Grant Teaff; head coach, Baylor University 1972–1992; executive director, American Football Coaches Association; College Football Hall of Fame

"Those in the limelight often suffer when the lights go out. Randy's addiction may have started in professional football, but it's not unlike the story of any of us who have struggled to find our identity and rudder outside of our careers. This book is a true and riveting account of redemption from someone who barely made it out alive from his addiction—yet is now one of the strongest advocates and fellow interventionists. Thank you for your honesty, Randy. Your story will help many."

—Jennifer Gimenez; American supermodel, actress, reality television personality, and addiction recovery advocate

"Randy told me once that he would have liked to have played for me. And I, of course, would have liked to have coached him. By reading this book, it's obvious why: he never gives up! It's okay to get knocked down, but you must rise again. Life after football knocked Randy down, but he didn't stay there. And when he got up, he used his experience to help others. What more could a coach ask for?"

—Jackie Sherrill; head coach, Texas A&M 1982–1988; head coach, Mississippi State 1991–1903

"I've seen athletes over the years who wanted to be great but were unwilling to do the necessary hard work. Recovery is similar. Some want to be sober—but are unwilling to do what it takes. Not only did Randy do the work, but his story is the perfect example of the fruits of recovery. This book is one of those fruits!"

—"Sudden" Sam McDowell; MLB pitcher, Cleveland Indians 1961–1975; six times MLB All-Star; author, *The Saga of Sudden Sam*

"I played during the same time as Randy and shared his conference, and in fact faced his team twice a year. I know first-hand the pressures he faced to stay on the field. I also know the play-at-all-costs mentality that existed then. Randy accurately describes the dark side of the NFL, and what many were and still are willing to do to be the best. Great job, my NFL brother!"

—Eric Hipple; NFL QB, Detroit Lions 1980–1989; mental health advocate; author, *Real Men Do Cry*

"As a former Olympic swimmer with three Gold Medals, I know what it takes to be the best. I also know what it's like when we are no longer that athlete who we worked so hard to become. When the cheering stops, life gets confusing, and sometimes we struggle with finding who we are in this new role. Randy reinvented himself by using his experience to help others. I applaud him and countless others who have found a way to stay clean and sober one day at a time. I'm one of them! A great read."

—Carrie Bates; three-time Gold Medalist swimmer, 1984 Olympics

"I've studied and written about teams that consistently perform at the highest level. Randy's well-told story is captivating, demonstrating how teams both on and off the field are necessary for strength and support, especially during our darkest times."

—John Ross, PhD, MBA; assistant professor of leadership, strategy, and entrepreneurship, Indiana University Southeast; author, *Team Unity: A Leader's Guide to Unlocking Extraordinary Potential*

"As a former competitive three-event show skier and barefoot water skier, I can relate to Randy's injuries and also his drive to be the best. Being the best often comes with a price. As an interventionist, I also can relate to the lifesaving tool that we have to help someone struggling. The intervention that Randy and Lydia show is typical of the groundwork and execution of a successful intervention. I'm thankful that we can create a 'bottom' for someone before they hit their real bottom, from which many never recover. This book is powerful!"

—Tim Ryan; advocate; A&E's *Dope Man*; author, *From Dope to Hope*; founder, A Man in Recovery Foundation

OFF CENTER

OFF CENTER

A MEMOIR OF ADDICTION, RECOVERY, AND REDEMPTION IN PROFESSIONAL FOOTBALL

RANDY GRIMES

SPIRITUS COMMUNICATIONS

ISBN: 978-0-9845917-6-3 (paperback)
ISBN: 978-0-9845917-8-7 (hardcover)
ISBN: 978-0-9845917-7-0 (e-book)

Library of Congress Control Number: 2022900011

Edited by Jocelyn Carbonara
Proofread by Amy Weinstein
Cover design by Phil Davis
Interior design by Chip Thrasher

Published by Spiritus Communications, Hillsborough, NC, USA

This book is dedicated to the true heroes of recovery—including the warriors fighting addiction and their supporters; my own family, especially my precious wife whose grace, patience, and mercy were beyond earthly bounds; and my heavenly Father who never abandoned me.

FOREWORD

MIKE DITKA

Every NFL player lives with pain resulting from innumerable brutal hits on the gridiron. Players quickly learn that to make it, they need physical and mental toughness to play through that pain. If they don't find a way, other guys will snatch their positions in a heartbeat.

To keep players in the game, team doctors mend their injuries and manage their pain. Once a player leaves the game for good, however, they're on their own. But that doesn't mean the pain goes away. For too many players, the medication they took to stay on the field follows them into retirement.

Sometimes, the medicine that "cures" turns into a poison that kills. Ask Randy Grimes, who played center for the Tampa Bay Buccaneers for a decade. In 1992, Randy left pro football with more than just accolades and injuries. He'd also gained an addiction to pills that cost him relationships, jobs, homes, cars, and nearly his life.

Unfortunately, Randy is not alone. The CDC reported more than 100,000 deaths in the twelve-month period ending in April 2021, a 28.5 percent increase from the previous twelve-month period. And many new heroin users started by misusing prescription pain medicine.

The good news is that no one needs to struggle alone. Randy refused to be defined by his addiction, and he got help.

I applaud Randy's NFL career. But I'm even prouder of his courage to tell his story: that of a ten-year starting center getting knocked completely *off center* by his addiction.

Today, Randy offers hope to athletes and non-athletes struggling with addiction. I've witnessed Randy guide countless people from despair to redemption.

In September 2019, I inducted Randy Grimes into the Mike Ditka's Gridiron Greats Hall of Fame for his fight against addiction—a feat requiring as much mental toughness as playing pro ball. In football, we say, "You are only as good as your team." I'm glad Randy is part of my team. He proves that together, we can beat addiction. This story goes beyond football, fortune, and fame. It shows what it's like to be caught up in a deadly fixation on drugs, and offers a playbook for getting back in the game of life.

Mike Ditka
1961 NFL Rookie of the Year
1968 College Football Hall of Fame
1988 Pro Football Hall of Fame
1985 and 1988 NFL Coach of the Year
Board of Directors, Gridiron Greats

PREFACE

Baseball may be America's pastime, but from the fall to the middle of winter, every home in the US has at least one football fan. Starting at a young age, I played both sports. But by the time I entered high school, football became an extension of my religion and life itself.

Many boys can relate to loving football. However, loving the game doesn't necessarily mean it's easy to play at the highest level. For every ten thousand high school boys that play, only about nine of them, or .09 percent, make it into the NFL.

Top players need the right genes—ones that give them the size, speed, and strength the game requires. On top of genes, it takes discipline, training, and coaching to reach peak performance. Finally, it takes a good deal of luck.

I guess that makes me lucky.

Football players today better understand the risks involved in playing such a brutal sport, especially long-term. Almost every player I've known talks about how hard it is to get out of bed each morning due to deep bruises and aching joints. Today's players are savvier to the risks.

Like many athletes, I measured my self-worth based on how

well I played. As I evolved from rookie to seasoned veteran, the physical blows left me with perpetual pain and discomfort. The longer I played, the more I feared a career-ending injury, threatening not only my livelihood, but my identity.

I planned to do whatever necessary to stay on the field. My resolve led me to pain medications and tranquilizers. I needed sleep to recuperate after each game, so I justified the pills. Besides, they were handed out by team doctors and trainers who I trusted. If those drugs could keep me on the field, I'd take them.

But even before the big lights faded and my football career folded shut, I kept a secret from everyone: I'd started taking pills throughout the day, every day.

My little secret wouldn't stay hidden forever, nor would my lucky streak continue.

What started off as pain relief became an obsession that nearly destroyed all that I touched in the process.

This is my story of having it all while playing the sport I love, losing almost everything, and finding redemption and hope—before it was too late.

Note to the reader:

This book intertwines two stories—of my life and an intervention I conducted with my wife, Lydia. To help you navigate, each chapter heading will indicate which storyline is being covered.

Randy Grimes

INTRODUCTION
THE INTERVENTION

*"I love that this morning's sunrise does not define itself
by last night's sunset."*

—STEVE MARABOLI

December 20, 2018

Rain pelted the windshield in waves, forcing the black Ford Explorer to slow along the curved country road. The couple remained quiet, like they had for much of their long drive since landing in Atlanta a few hours earlier.

A green sign announced they were nearing Coosa, an unincorporated community outside of Rome, Georgia. Rain turned to a slushy mix, as the car pulled off, across from a short gravel driveway beside a small house. When the man shut off the headlights, their vehicle faded into the surroundings.

"Is this it?" the lean woman asked softly, turning her head to see if there were other homes nearby.

"Must be," the large man responded. "I know she has a red car, and I guess that one could be red. And look." He pointed to a mangled pickup behind the car in the driveway. "There's the wrecked truck."

The two sat in silence while scanning. Just behind the vehicles, they could make out the remains of an old fence that had once been painted white. Beyond the few remaining pickets, they could see nothing but what looked like the shadow of a large tree—flat on the ground, with branches reaching up to the sky like a mangled scarecrow.

The ranch-style home looked like an old double-wide with a small, overhanging porch rigged over the front door. Through a window in the door, a faint yellow light shone. While many of the homes they'd passed on their drive displayed festive Christmas lights and decorations, this home looked stark. Instead of garlands twirling around the door, this home had strips of faded paint peeling from the siding, twisting with each new wind gust.

"Are you sure you're up for this?" the man asked his passenger, looking into her piercing, green eyes which sparkled in the dim light from the dash.

The woman bit her lower lip and hesitated. "I don't know if I ever *feel* ready," she said at last.

The man reached his enormous hand into his coat pocket and took out his phone. After keying a short message, he placed his phone on the dash and looked at the house again, until his phone beeped.

He looked at his phone briefly and then turned back to the woman in the passenger seat.

"This is the place. Let's do this," he said while unlatching his seatbelt.

"Wait," the woman responded. "We can't go alone."

Had anyone been watching the couple in the car, they might have been surprised to see the two holding hands, closing their eyes, and praying in the darkness.

Had anyone still been watching less than twelve hours later, they might be even more surprised to see the large man put a duffle bag in the back of his car while glancing over his shoulders. Who knows what an onlooker would have thought seeing the man and woman walk through the doorway with a tall, thin, scruffy-looking man sandwiched between them, as they shuffled to the car before driving away, just as the sun broke on the horizon.

CHAPTER ONE

THE INTERVENTION

"Be completely humble and gentle; be patient,
bearing with one another in love."

—EPHESIANS 4:2, *NEW INTERNATIONAL VERSION*

December 17, 2018

My wife, Lydia, keeps sensible hours, so she kissed me goodnight around ten o'clock and headed to bed.

I envy the way sleep comes easily to her. That's not the case with me. After years of taking and giving abuse playing football, I usually feel the most joint discomfort when the house gets still and my day winds down.

While I no longer heap physical pain on my body since leaving football, I still absorb a good deal of emotional fatigue from my work in the drug and alcohol treatment industry. After a long day of helping others deal with their crises, I usually end up flipping channels for a few hours, instead of cuddling with my beautiful wife. I call it *Randy Time.*

Just before 11:00 p.m., my cell phone rang, and I muted the television.

"Hello, this is Randy Grimes," I answered, not recognizing the number, or even area code.

"Hi," a woman's voice replied. Her Southern accent made her greeting sound more like, "Ha."

"Is this Randy Grimes?"

"This is Randy Grimes. How can I help?" I responded as I switched off the TV.

"Well, my name is Wilma, and I live in Georgia," the woman answered. "I don't know what you do, but my friend gave me your name. Do you know Laverne?" I recalled a woman whose daughter, Alana, I'd helped get into treatment two years earlier.

"I sure do," I told her. "Are you having problems? Or is a loved one struggling with an addiction?" I asked.

"Well, that's the thing," Wilma said. "I don't know if it's a problem or not. It's not me; it's my son, Bobby. He lives with me, since he split up with his wife. That's Julia, and she thinks Bobby has a drinking problem. That's why they separated. And now my daughter, Allison, thinks Bobby has a problem, 'cause two days ago he borrowed Teddy's truck—that's Allison's husband—and wrecked it. And that's when Bobby got a DUI, too."

"In an ideal world, how can I help Bobby?" I asked Wilma, trying to keep track of the names and events.

I'd been doing this long enough to know how to get to the point, while still showing my genuine care.

"I know that Bobby likes to drink, but...." After the *but,* Wilma shared a slew of reasons why she wasn't sure Bobby had a *real* drinking problem.

She underplayed Bobby's drinking. She minimized his two DUIs: "Well, Bobby was depressed, because he'd just lost another job."

"How many jobs has he lost?" I asked.

"Well, that was the second job he lost when he got his first DUI," Wilma replied. Then she corrected herself. "No, he got his first DUI after he lost his third job. Now I remember."

Wilma made Bobby's wrecking of his brother-in-law's truck sound like it was the truck's fault. She even added that "Bobby is as careful a driver as I've seen. He just wasn't familiar with that truck is all, since he'd just borrowed it that day." It didn't matter to Wilma that Bobby got arrested at the scene when the breathalyzer showed a .15 blood alcohol reading.

Wilma shared that her grandmother's jewelry went missing after Bobby moved home, and that Bobby's wife threw him out for driving their daughter to school with alcohol on his breath.

Still, Wilma wasn't sure that Bobby had a *real* drinking problem.

"You see," Wilma related sadly, "Bobby's father, Rusty, left when us when Bobby was in high school. He just up and left. Poor Bobby was devastated. Rusty used to take Bobby hunting and fishing. They were very close. And I don't think Bobby ever recovered from that, you know?"

Wilma shared that Rusty died in a car accident less than two years after leaving the family.

"Bobby played baseball, and he was real good. First base, since he's tall with long arms. I used to watch him play every time I could get off work," Wilma said proudly. "And he made good grades, too. Honor roll, even. Got a good scholarship for college to study business, 'cause he was so smart."

According to Wilma, she knew that Bobby drank in college, but she swore he just drank like everyone else. She also told me that he found college hard, and his grades slipped.

Classes got harder? I wondered to myself. *Or maybe drinking took center stage.*

After college, Bobby worked as an accountant at a

plumbing supply company nearby. The owner, Gary, was an old family friend who took Bobby under his wing—personally and professionally.

Bobby met his wife-to-be, Julia, at an office party a few years later. Julia had crashed the party with a friend who worked there. The couple quickly became inseparable and married two years later.

Bobby, the rising star at his company, and Julia, a nurse at the local hospital, brought in good money. After a year of renting, they bought a nice home in Rome, Georgia, where they both worked. Not long after that, Bobby started buying things to cement his status as an adult and man: a male boxer mix for companionship and a four-wheeler for fun.

The dog proved to be a good addition. But the four-wheeler turned out to be nothing but trouble. Wilma told me that the end of the four-wheeler came when Bobby pushed it too hard in a turn while driving too fast. Bobby and the machine tumbled, with the machine landing on top of him.

That accident messed up Bobby's shoulder, and he needed two surgeries and many visits to physical therapy to regain motion. In the meantime, Bobby took prescribed pain medicine.

Pain. If I had a nickel for every time I heard of someone's addiction starting with alcohol or pain medication to cope with pain, emotional or physical...

My buddy, Tim, suffered from dyslexia and other learning disabilities. But when he self-medicated with alcohol and drugs, he felt "normal" for the first time.

Another friend, Scott, was a crisis counselor who worked with cases of abuse and neglect. After being up close and personal with three tragic deaths in rapid succession, all involving drugs and/or alcohol, he blamed himself. Years later, he turned to the bottle to drown his ongoing grief.

Another friend and hockey player, Nick, went into the hospital with kidney stones. After repeated surgeries, he became addicted to pain meds before turning to heroin.

I wondered what part of Bobby's addiction was triggered by his accident and subsequent pain.

CHAPTER TWO

RANDY'S STORY

"If a man's from Texas, he will tell you. If he's not, why embarrass him by asking?"

—JOHN GUNTHER

Two people can start in very different worlds but still manage to end up in the same place.

To hear Wilma tell it, her family's connection to Georgia went back more than two hundred years, whereas my world took root in Tyler, Texas.

Also known as the "Rose capital of the world," Tyler gave rise to NFL Hall of Famer with the Houston Oilers and New Orleans Saints, Earl Campbell. Campbell went by "the Tyler Rose" for his colorful, brilliant moves as a running back. (I later would be called "the Tyler Thorn" for my brutal attacks as a center.)

My parents were native Texans, so being a Texan is not only in my nature and a source of pride, but it's in my blood.

My dad had served as a law enforcement officer in Crandall, outside of Dallas. Crandall was a small town and held onto good old American—and Texas—values. But when my dad heard about the newly expanded Tyler Police Department, he went. Tyler was bigger, with more opportunity, where he was eventually promoted to detective before working in adult probation and retiring as a parole officer.

As far as my mom, well, she happily did whatever Dad wanted her to do. She didn't take any job outside of our home until I entered elementary school, when she worked as a cashier. When I was in junior high, she worked in my school as the principal's assistant. From junior high through high school, I could never get away with a single thing without Momma finding out!

My mom was loving, supportive, and present. Growing up, Momma put a freshly cooked meal on the table every evening and demanded that everybody eat together and had us in church every Sunday. I am grateful today for that. And she not only attended every game, but she also attended every practice.

And talk about beautiful. Momma was and is one of the most attractive women I've ever seen. She set the bar extremely high.

When she was a child, my mom was so poor that she and her siblings would ride in the back of a dump truck to school each day. Her dad worked for Ford Motors, and every weekend, he would go coon hunting—and would often drink. Granny could tell if he was drunk when he got home by the way he wore his hat. During the week, if he came home drunk, she would put him to bed before the kids saw him.

Momma did well in school, but she also excelled in basketball, something few girls played then. Many members of her family served proudly in the military, some even dying in combat—including her beloved brother, Sam.

I have one sister and one brother. My sister, Roxanne, came first, followed a couple of years later by my brother, Dickey. I came along two years later, July 20, 1960. We were born two years apart like clockwork, almost as if my parents followed a schedule.

Don't bother asking me how much I weighed or how tall I was at birth. I don't remember. But according to my mom, I wasn't big or small, short or tall. Just *normal*.

I couldn't ask for a better sister than Roxanne. She loved me and Dickey, rarely treating us like the bratty younger brothers we acted like at times. Being four years older and the only girl, she found her own interests and made her own friends. By the time I hit my teen years, I was thrilled when Roxanne brought her friends over, because I wanted to date them all! Roxanne could dance like a professional and did well in drill team. She was also very smart. If something involved brains and school, Roxanne was there.

My brother, Dickey, who showed great athleticism from an early age, got involved in sports, and served as my mentor and role model. He made me competitive, driving a desire to be as good or better than he was in sports. Even with two years between us, many of our friends overlapped, because we ran in the same circles. It didn't matter if we were playing neighborhood sports or sandlot games, we were together.

Dickey meant the world to me. I looked up to him on many levels. He was good-looking, great in sports, always had the coolest cars, worked hard, and everybody loved him.

As much as I looked up to Dickey, the strongest role model in my life was my favorite coach, my dad. Dad wasn't a big guy. Well, he was probably 6'2", but he wasn't big compared to Dickey and me. I respected Dad not for his size or athleticism, but for his calm, Tom Landry-like demeanor and ability to motivate others.

Until seventh grade, Dad coached me in every sport I played. His lessons stuck with me longer than anything I learned from any professional coach I had after him.

And I'm not alone. Recently, I sat with a bunch of guys from my old Little League team that Dad coached. I got choked up hearing those guys—my age—talking about how Dad never gave up on them, encouraged them with his every action, and turned our ragtag team into a great ball team that went undefeated. They didn't remember who hit what game's winning run, or even who played what position. What stuck with them were vivid memories of my dad smiling, nodding, and gently slapping them with encouragement on their backs.

For Dad, though, winning wasn't what made the world go round. Dad was all about relationships.

One guy on our team, Kevin, struggled to hit the ball. Dad never gave up on him. Kevin tried to drop his bat and walk away from the plate, but Dad said, "Hey, Buddy! We've got time. Shake it off! Swing again!"

Dad stuck with Kevin, until we all heard a loud crack as the ball was launched deep into the outfield.

"That's what I mean, son! That's how you do it!" From my dad's enthusiasm, you might think that Kevin was of his own flesh. But that was just Dad's way. He treated everyone with kindness, respect, and encouragement.

As much as Dad loved police work, I think his calling was to coach. Looking back, I wonder if Dad always wanted to be a great athlete but lacked the opportunity. When he had the chance to bring out greatness in others, you could feel his passion, even in celebrating someone's attitude or sign of improvement in their play.

But Dad was also tough at times. In fourth grade, I played flag football barefoot. Don't ask me why. It's just what I did. One day it was cold as heck, and I walked out on the field wearing shorts and no shoes.

When someone stepped on my feet with cleats, Dad walked out onto the field, threw me over his shoulder, and carried me off. Fifty-plus years later, the humiliation still turns my face red. Then, to make matters worse, he stopped halfway back to the sideline, walked back into the huddle—with me still dangling over his shoulders—to call the next play. Utter humiliation.

I now know that this was Dad's way of showing me that he would take care of me as his top priority.

But he would also take care of his responsibilities, like coaching that team.

At the time, though, I thought, *Um, Dad, isn't there a better way to handle this? Do you think you could just let me walk off the field with a shred of dignity?*

I know I was lucky to have my family. We didn't have loads of money, but we had each other. And we had sports. Whenever one of us kids wanted or needed something for school or an extracurricular activity, my parents found a way to fund it. When one of us joined a team, whether sports for Dickey and me, or dance and academics for Roxanne, both of my parents were there.

Even my dad's father, who I knew as Papaw, came out to watch me play football. He never missed a game.

But Papaw was eccentric. Dad told me that as a young man, Papaw drank too much whiskey, especially after his workdays. Today we'd call him an alcoholic; back then he was known as an irascible drunk. He was the constable in Crandall. He'd drink a lot on duty, and the family would get calls.

He also had a painting job, and it wasn't uncommon to see his police car at a job site where he was painting, drunk. He also hung wallpaper. My mom said he once papered an entire kitchen with a bright, goose print. Thanks to large amounts of Wild Turkey, he hung all those geese flying upside down.

Papaw would take my dad when he was little and disappear for days on drinking binges. His wife, Mamaw, never knew where they were.

Papaw would go to bars and not leave until Mamaw dragged him home. According to family legend, Mamaw got so mad at Papaw for drinking one night that while he laid passed out in the bed, she sewed him up between two bedsheets and beat him with a broomstick. Back then, people might have called Mamaw crazy; but today, I'd say she possessed strong convictions and a willingness to go to any extreme to help her husband get sober. Which he eventually did.

I don't think Mamaw's "therapy" had anything to do with him putting the bottle down, but in hindsight, I wish I'd asked him what made him quit. His secret may have helped me.

When Papaw watched me play, he'd come out to each game, but he'd stand far away from the field, viewing from a distance. He'd never say anything to me and rarely even looked my way. A couple of times he nodded or spit in my general direction, but that was it. Then he'd leave without saying a word, like a thief in the night. We might have dinner with Papaw at our house a few hours later, but he wouldn't mention one thing about how I'd played. It was enough for me that he came out to show interest and support. But yeah, that was eccentric.

One of my fondest memories of Papaw was when he took me out to Bellwood Lake just to teach me to shoot rubber bands. He walked me into the reeds and showed me how to hook a band around my finger, aim, and shoot. That was some fun stuff.

"See, little buddy," Papaw told me. "We don't need a fancy boat or money to have fun. We have a lake, a couple of pockets of rubber bands, and even a few dragonflies for targets," he said as he gestured to the dragonflies bobbing up and down on the reeds.

Don't worry about the dragonflies. We never actually hit one, which was probably predesigned, but the excitement came from spending the day with Papaw.

I later found out this was one of his favorite drinking spots, although I never witnessed it. He was probably good at hiding it, because he lived with Mamaw.

Papaw didn't go to church. Well, he went to the church

building, but he never actually went inside. Each Sunday, he'd drive Mamaw to the service and wait alone in his car until it was time to go home. I heard more than one fight between Papaw and Mamaw about his resistance to organized religion.

That indifference spread to the next generation. My father didn't go to church either, but my mom did. Each week, she'd dress herself and us kids in our finest clothes to attend services.

We weren't united as a family while worshipping in the Lord's house each Sunday, but we were united in watching football. Every game became a family event.

One Sunday, Mom asked Dad if he'd come to church with us. Dad thought a moment before answering.

"Gay, I'll make a deal with you. If the Lord gives Randy a football scholarship, I'll go to church with you every Sunday for the rest of my life."

"Richard, you're not making a deal with just me," Mom held up a finger for emphasis. "You're making a bargain with God. And the two of us will hold you to it!"

In addition to being a wonderful mother, my mom was a strong prayer warrior. Years later, I would learn just how actively she prayed. No matter what was going on with me, she grew calluses on her knees—either begging God to intercede or thanking him for his interception.

Mixed into all the positive experiences is one memory that nearly changed my life. At the lake with my family one day, I started looking for new adventure, as any eight-year-old might. When I saw a paddleboat on a small dock, without saying anything, I jumped in and took myself for a little joyride—away from the shore into deeper waters.

I don't remember exactly what I was reaching for, but I stretched my small arm out to grab something that felt important at the time. When I shifted my weight, the boat reacted, and I lost my balance. Before I knew it, I was overboard, sinking silently beneath the slippery surface.

By the time I knew where I was, I was trapped underneath the boat, the depths calling for me. I screamed out in desperation as I flailed my arms and legs, trying to release myself. But the water muted my voice to all ears but my own. My lungs cried out for oxygen.

Since I was only eight, it didn't take long for my short life to flash before my eyes. Then my arms weakened, and my head clouded as my vision started to flicker.

Finally, by some miracle, my hand felt the edge of the rigid boat. I grasped it tightly with my small fingers, pulling myself as quickly as I could towards open water. As my body rushed through the water, eventually shooting above the surface, I sucked in big gulps of air—undoubtedly screaming for help.

Even as an eight-year-old, I knew I'd cheated death.

Climbing back onto the boat as soon as my strength returned, my tears mixed with the water. I continued to pant for several minutes. When I felt ready to paddle my way to shore, I looked around, shocked at how far out I'd gone from land.

Paddling back, I felt no embarrassment about how I'd flailed while trapped underwater. When you're drowning, you don't care how cool you look. You either find your breath, or you die.

At age eight, I couldn't know how this terror and desperation would revisit me.

CHAPTER THREE

THE INTERVENTION

December 17, 2018

I learned from Wilma that shortly after Bobby's accident, Julia gave birth to their only child, Anna, who was now six.

Wilma confided in me that she was more worried about Bobby taking those pills than drinking. But she was especially worried about him mixing the two.

As Wilma continued, something dawned on her.

"Come to think of it, Bobby didn't have problems until the accident. I mean, he drank, but he never got in trouble." She asked after a pause, "Do you think that accident may have messed up his head?"

To myself, I wondered if that accident may have taken him from drinker to heavy drinker, or heavy drinker into problem drinker. *And then when you add pills...*, I thought.

Both Bobby and Julia were raised as "good Southern Baptists," as Wilma called them, and she assured me that Bobby, Julia, and Ann attended church nearly every week.

"Of course," Wilma conceded, "Bobby hasn't gone to church much since his accident. But some of that," she continued, "is because those pills make him sleepy. And he worked so hard during the week that he was just too tired to go."

Sometimes we tell ourselves what we want to be true. Wilma wanted to believe that Bobby and his family attended church every Sunday, but it had been six years. Wilma stood at the threshold of denial and truth, a place I knew well. I also knew a big part of the work ahead for me would be to nudge Wilma into accepting that Bobby's addiction wreaked havoc on more lives than just Bobby's.

At the end of the call, I told Wilma I'd be happy to come see if maybe Bobby thought it was time to get help. I suggested that I might bring my wife, Lydia, too.

The longer Wilma spoke—or I should say, the longer Wilma heard herself talk—the more convinced she became that Bobby might have slid past *one who suffers from depression and abandonment issues* into *one who has a real drinking problem.*

Wilma gave me names and numbers of those who most loved Bobby. I let her know how I would stage an intervention with the help of those on the list. I told her that starting the next morning, I'd call to see if they would help. The following day, I'd fly to Georgia with my wife and drive to Wilma's home. From there, we'd head to Allison's—Bobby's sister's house—to meet, assuming Allison would participate. If not, we'd just meet in Lydia's and my hotel room. And then, in just three days, we'd do an intervention with Bobby.

"The rest," I explained, "I'll discuss when we meet face-to-face as a group."

After I hung up, I looked at the list. Then I wrote up a short to-do list to start on in the morning.

I put the TV back on and flipped channels mindlessly for a few minutes, but my mind was too keyed up. Finally, I gave up and went to bed.

Sliding under the sheets by Lydia, I felt her radiant, gentle warmth. Staring up at the dark, I processed my call with Wilma.

I'd been fielding calls like this about every two weeks for the last few years. The names were different. People called from as far away as California (and I live in Florida) and as close as a ten-minute drive. The calls weren't always about drinking. Half the time they were about drug misuse. And sometimes instead of a mother, the call would come from a wife, husband, father, sibling, or even close friend.

But change the name, address, drug of choice, and relationship of the person calling, and I'd heard this story hundreds of times. And each time, I related—with a twinge of pain, and even more gratitude.

I rolled over, putting an arm around my wife to squeeze her gently. She didn't wake, but she pulled my arm closer and clung to me. I buried my nose in her hair. *Thank you, Lord, for bringing me this amazing woman,* I nearly whispered under my breath.

I listened to Lydia's breathing for a few minutes and eventually fell asleep in synch with her rhythm.

That night, I dreamed desperate dreams. In my dream, I couldn't find Lydia, and I felt utterly alone. Everything around me looked dark. Then I heard a voice that sounded more like an animal than a human. And even though I couldn't make out its words, I felt something just short of terror.

CHAPTER FOUR

RANDY'S STORY

"Drunkenness is nothing but voluntary madness."

—SENECA

My life did not start out anywhere near addiction. As a teen, I was thriving.

College football scouts typically show up right after spring training of junior year. As I entered my senior year, I knew that scouts could be in the crowd watching. And if I played well, they might look at my game tapes and stats.

One day in the locker room, my coach pulled me aside.

"Randy, scouts are out there today. You better play the best damn game of your life!"

Yeah, actually, that never happened. The coaches didn't know from one minute to the next who might be in the stands. But the coaches stressed two things: one, *every game matters*, and two, *the game you are about to play should be better than the one before.*

I lived for that kind of pressure. I'd been preparing for a

shot at a college scholarship since fourth grade. I played my senior year knowing that every moment mattered to my future, and I was prepared to push myself to my breaking point to land at a good college.

It turns out, several scouts did come to watch our team play. But they weren't there for me. They came to scout my two teammates, Kent Townsend and Andy Lacey. As luck had it, while watching my two teammates, those scouts discovered me and took an interest.

Many good events in my life happened by chance: being in the right place, right position, right time, and surrounded by the right people. Even before my awareness of Divine Providence, God opened the doors I needed to run through.

In February, after the season finished, I visited most colleges in the Southwest Conference. Rice and Baylor made me scholarship offers. And I was biased. My sister Roxanne had graduated from Baylor the year before, but she still lived on campus while her husband finished grad school. That made my decision very easy: "I'm going to Baylor!" I canceled all other planned visits.

My teammate, Kent, also accepted a scholarship with Baylor, and our other outstanding teammate, Andy, got snatched up by TCU.

Remember the promise Dad made to Mom about going to church if I got a football scholarship? After Baylor recruited me, Dad never missed a Sunday service. Football got Dad more interested in knowing a God who heard prayers, especially about important topics like ballgames. As a result, Dad became a born-again believer.

Football—and now God too—served to knit together the Grimes household. We became an unbreakable unit around both the gridiron and church.

Outside of football, I worked several jobs and stayed social.

As my eighteenth birthday approached, that social life included finding alcohol.

Part of my desire to drink came from being a typical, stupid eighteen-year-old. Another part of it might be that I never saw my parents drink, so curiosity came into play. I wanted to know what I might be missing.

So while my parents didn't drink—*I had to try.*

Clay was my best friend throughout much of high school. We did everything together, as we were into all the same activities: sports, girls, and calves. No, not the calves on girls. I'm talking grade A baby cow kind of calves that we showed at Future Farmers of America. Of course, the reason we showed calves didn't have to do with a love of husbandry; it was a way to meet some cute farm girls.

Clay's dad was a dentist, and I spent a lot of time at their house. When Clay got interested in showing calves, he got me into it too, and we showed at livestock shows across the region. His dad actually later bought my calf.

And it was just a matter of time before Clay and I started drinking together.

We lived in a dry county. Back then, dry counties were common throughout Texas. Obviously, that's changed quite a bit.

I had just turned eighteen, the legal drinking age back then in Texas. To celebrate, my friends were planning one hell of a bash that weekend on a lake.

Clay and I cut school to make our first-ever beer run. Our friends provided the cash, and I provided the legal ID. We drove to Coffee City, the next county over. I walked into the liquor store, oblivious to the TV cameras all around. Inside, a crew worked a couple of cameras so big that each operator needed another guy just to hold a separate battery pack.

So stupid me goes strolling into the liquor store, trying to look like I'd done this a thousand times. As I approached the counter to secure my purchase, I started listening to one of the reporters.

"How much cash did the assailant take?" she asked the clerk.

Lucky me had entered a liquor store to buy beer right after it had been robbed!

While I tried to look invisible—which is really hard when you're 6'4" and weigh over 225 pounds—one camera shot customers in the store to use as B roll for the news broadcast.

So the first time I ever tried to buy beer, I ended up on the five o' clock news. That could have earned me bragging rights with the guys—like I was some sort of news star for a second—except that my parents happened to watch that newscast. I'm pretty sure Dad wanted to beat the hell out of me. I'd embarrassed him like Papaw used to do. Fortunately for me, he just lectured me pretty hard about cutting class and drinking instead of throwing me over his shoulder again or bending me over his knee.

A month later, Clay and I went to stay in a little coastal town called Sinton. Away from our parents, we figured we'd get our drink on. Where we had failed to score booze the first time, we determined to make up for it away from any parental controls.

Have you ever had rum punch? That stuff is evil. At least when you drink straight whiskey, the burn in your throat serves as a drinking "speed bump." You can drink only so much before that whiskey wants to find daylight in the direction of the nearest commode or alley.

Anyway, back to rum punch. When something tastes like Kool-Aid, you may belt down glass after glass so quickly that you don't feel the effects until BOOM! You're drunk off your butt.

Which is what happened to me at a local VFW hall, where

Clay and I drank that night. Eighteen years old and intoxicated on a dangerous combination of hubris and liquor, in no time we ended up fighting with some locals.

Picture those saloon fight scenes in old Westerns, with chairs getting smashed over heads and tables flying in all directions. That bar in Sinton broke into that kind of ugly, barroom brawl. What started off with insults and shoves turned into chairs, tables, bottles, and fists flying. When the police arrived, they grabbed the biggest, drunkest, loudest guy in the bunch, and threw him in jail.

That guy would be me.

I was eighteen, stinking drunk for the first time in my life, experiencing bed-spins while standing, and feeling like a volcano was ready to erupt from my being. So when I got thrown into a jail cell, I naively thought the worst was behind me.

It wasn't.

For many people, drinking has three stages: laughing, fighting, and passing out. Having finished stages one and two, I planned on exploring stage three. I jumped onto the closest bunk to pass out for the night. Unfortunately, the bed already had an occupant, who jumped up—screaming and throwing lightning-fast punches at my face. Of course, I didn't understand what he was saying because he spoke in Spanish, but I gathered he thought that my intentions were amorous. He and his buddies declined "my offer" by taking turns beating the crap out of me. That went on for what seemed like hours, and in between blows, I looked around for help. A guard sitting outside the cell looked up briefly, then went back to his magazine. After that, I took my beating in silence. The only noises coming from our little cell were the sounds of fists hitting my face and feet slamming into my sides.

Both my eyes swelled shut, and a couple of ribs felt broken

or at least badly bruised. But I didn't give those guys the satisfaction of crying out for help. After a while, I think their hands started to hurt from hitting me so hard. Eventually, their blows and insults (or, I should say, what I can only guess were insults) faded.

A metal picnic table sat in the middle of the room. I crawled up on top of that slab of cold steel, spending the rest of my night watching my back to make sure they didn't return.

And that's when I knew I could never be a successful heavy drinker.

The next morning, I stood before the judge, feeling like a gutted piñata. I looked like hell, and I'm sure I didn't smell like a rose either.

"Get the hell out of Sinton, Mr. Grimes. And don't let me see your face around here again, you hear?" The judge dismissed my charges. Perhaps he felt like I'd gotten a tough enough sentence in jail the night before that he showed me mercy. I later learned that Clay's grandparents knew the judge, so that helped too.

That little incident never went on my record.

My parents never said a word about it—because they never knew. In fact, they still don't know. I'm still a little boy when it comes to wanting to please my parents. So Momma, if you're reading this, I'm sorry I never told you. I didn't want to disappoint you. And I know it took me a while, but I've learned my lesson.

Looking back, I didn't think that one ugly, drunken chapter in my life would be a prelude to anything worse. I just considered myself your typical eighteen-year-old—not knowing my limits, getting pig drunk, and fighting like I had something to prove.

Alcohol would never be my drug of choice. Truth is, I didn't even smoke cigarettes. I tried to smoke pot a couple of times, but I couldn't inhale. My lungs couldn't take it. The smoke burned and made me cough.

But chewing tobacco became my thing. I started in eighth grade and chewed with the best of them. I hid a can of dip next to my ankle in my cowboy boot. I'm a Texan, remember? No self-respecting Texan would wear tennis shoes. My junior high vice principal made it his mission to crack down on kids using chewing tobacco. Every time he'd pass me in the hallway, he'd kick my ankles to see if I had a can of snuff in there. I always did. Yet he never busted me. He just kicked me hard enough to drive that can into my ankle bone. Maybe he was just doing his job. But at the time, I just thought he was just an asshole. Fact is, I wish he'd busted me harder. Maybe then I would have quit.

By the time I finished high school, my classmates voted me "most handsome" and "most favorite." I'm not sure how I got voted most handsome, but I'm guessing low standards played a big part.

But as far as most favorite, it's not hard to be a big fish in a small pond. People knew me from football, and my desire to make people laugh probably helped. I never set my sights on getting an academic scholarship, so with average grades, my teachers didn't love me for being a straight A student like they had my older sister. I excelled in classes that I enjoyed, like history, and I coasted in classes that bored me. Instead, most teachers liked me because I didn't cause trouble, and I had a way of smiling and joking to make them feel good about their jobs.

Popularity in high school in Tyler, Texas, was about fitting in. The cool kids wore blue jeans, Western shirts with mother-of-pearl snap buttons, and belt buckles so big they could serve as body armor. And, of course, cowboy boots. To be clear, we weren't cowboys. We were posers, drugstore cowboys at best. Yes, I showed calves, but remember, that wasn't about the cows.

During the summer before leaving for Baylor, I spent my

time on two things: getting ready for college football and earning money. Going from high school senior in a small town to a freshman at Baylor in the Southwest Conference of the NCAA Division I meant I'd be up against bigger, more experienced guys. I worked out, lifting weights and running. And I worked as an evening stock boy at JCPenney, a job I'd started after my freshman year in high school.

My parents taught me from birth that being a Grimes meant having a strong work ethic. When I didn't play football, I worked. In addition to JCPenney, I picked up as many odd jobs as I could each summer, all of them involving hard, manual labor. I laid carpet or did heavy lifting for a moving company. I even had a paper route as a kid every morning before school.

Throughout high school, I drove a blue '69 Camaro that my dad had bought for me. For college, my dad wanted me to have something more reliable to make that two-and-a-half-hour drive between Tyler and Waco. He was a car guy. He constantly changed out his ride. For a brief time, my mom had a lime green Pinto he bought her, the car I learned to drive in. Then he got her a '78 burnt-sienna Monte Carlo with a white vinyl roof. It ended up being too much car for her, so before I left for college, it became mine. I felt like I'd won the lottery.

Dad wasn't the only one getting me ready for college. For her part, my mother bought me about three thousand pairs of tube socks and Levi's. They were seconds. The stripes on the socks didn't match, and the crooked stitching on the Levi's made me look like I walked sideways. It wasn't until I got to school that I realized she didn't get me any underwear. While I had a lifetime supply of socks and jeans, I only had about a week's worth of underwear.

But none of that mattered. I'd finished high school, gotten a scholarship to Baylor, and would be driving a babe-magnet!

After hugging my parents, thanking them for everything

they'd done to support me and saying our final goodbyes, I started the Monte Carlo and began my next chapter.

Pulling away from Tyler, I knew that I couldn't have asked for a better family, upbringing, and childhood. As excited as I was to move forward, nostalgia already tugged at my heart. My childhood almost seemed to wave at me from the side yard, where our family had shared so many good times.

CHAPTER FIVE

THE INTERVENTION

"Home is the place where, when you have to go there,
they have to take you in."

—ROBERT FROST, *DEATH OF THE HIRED MAN*

December 18, 2018

I heard a scream more primitive and wild than any human voice. My chest tightened, my mouth moved to form words, and my whole body shook, gently at first but then with more persistence.

I awoke to Lydia shaking and reassuring me. I was drenched and panting, unable to tell if I were sweating out of fear, or if I had nearly drowned again.

Over coffee, I told Lydia about my call with Wilma.

"Really?" she asked. "I didn't even hear the phone ring."

Boy, do I admire her ability to sleep! I thought.

When I finished, I got around to my big ask.

"So if you're up for it, I thought we could both go," I smiled charmingly.

"I'd love to," Lydia said immediately. "Sounds like I can relate to Bobby's mom and wife."

"Yeah, that's what I was thinking," I nodded. "And I suppose I can relate to parts of Bobby."

While Lydia got busy packing and making our travel plans, I took out the list of eight names and phone numbers Wilma had given me the night before. From my scribbling, I studied it.

Wilma: Bobby's mom
Julia: Bobby's wife
Allison: Bobby's sister
Teddy: Bobby's brother-in-law, married to Allison
Robert: Bobby's grandfather, Wilma's dad
Gary: Bobby's former boss/family friend

I've worked interventions with a dozen or more names; other times, I've struggled to find even a handful of people willing to help. Bobby was lucky. From talking to Wilma, the people on this list all loved and wanted to support Bobby.

After a couple years of doing interventions, I developed a process for these calls. It all started with setting up my own home environment. I'd grab a big mug of hot, sweet coffee. Then I'd gather my notes, a notebook, a pen, and my phone. Then I'd settle into my overstuffed recliner in the living room.

From that chair, I can see my whole world: past, present, and future.

To my left, I see family treasures—like the violin-shaped antique clock that belonged to my father, which reminds me of where I came from and the man I most admire.

Immediately in front of me sits a trophy case with awards and game balls from some of my best—and worst—days. For years, football defined me. Above the trophy case, Lydia arranged family photos. Whenever I see the smiling faces of my stunning wife, dear children, and grandchildren, I'm brought back to my life's overwhelming value.

Finally, to the right of my chair is my balcony overlooking the sky-blue waters of Singer Island, Florida. This scene floods me with gratitude—and makes me want to help others feel it too, before it's too late.

Making calls for an intervention is a lot like making cold calls in sales. Except I'm not calling to sell people something they don't need. Instead, I'm offering to help them lose something I know they can't live with.

I always ask my initial contact to tell those on the list to expect my call. But when people reach a point of crisis, they have so much going on that they can't always follow through.

"Hi, my name is Randy Grimes. Is this (insert that person's name)?"

Unless the person says, "Yes, I've been expecting your call," I know I only have a couple of seconds before I get hung up on, taking me for a sales call or robocall.

So I usually speak quickly to let them know who I am.

In all my years, I've never had a person refuse to talk to me. People like helping others, even if they're angry with the person stuck in addictive behaviors. No one wants a loved one to be defined by his lowest moments.

Before placing the first call, I checked off Wilma's name. That little mark told me that I've already made some progress.

After taking a deep swig of coffee, I dialed Julia, Bobby's wife.

A female voice answered, "Hello?"

"Hi, my name is Randy Grimes. Is this...?" I began.

"Yes. Hi, Randy. Wilma told me you'd call." Julia spoke quickly, without waiting my response. "This is Julia. I'm tied up, but I really want to talk with you. Can I call you on my lunch hour when I'm alone?"

"Of course, Julia," I reassured her. "Just call me back at this number when you can. I'll be waiting. Bye-bye."

I wanted to award myself a half checkmark, but instead I dialed Bobby's grandfather, Robert, figuring he might be retired and able to talk freely.

"Hi, my name is Randy Grimes. Is this Robert?" I began again.

"Who?" an older gentleman's voice asked through the receiver loudly.

"My name is Randy Grimes. I am friends with your daughter, Wilma, Bobby's mother," I said more clearly and loudly.

"Oh, okay," the man returned. "Wilma called me this morning about you. So you want to do some sort of intervention with Bobby?"

"Yes, sir," I replied. "That's what I plan to do with your help."

"Such bullshit," Robert yelled. "Bobby just needs to man-up and quit drinking!"

"Well, sir, that would be great," I agreed. "But Wilma is worried that his drinking might be out of hand. Bobby may be an alcoholic. That's why I'm trying to help."

"Alcoholic?" Robert repeated sarcastically. "I used to drink until the bottle ached, and no one called me an alcoholic. They called me what I really was: a drunk. But one day I up and quit, just like that, and never looked back. I didn't need no intervention."

Old school, I thought.

"Congratulations!" I told Robert sincerely. "That's great. There is no wrong way to quit drinking," I assured him. "So what made you stop?" I asked.

"Willpower," Robert said proudly. "Mostly my wife's," he said with a deep laugh. "My wife was as strong as a mule and just as stubborn. What happened was, I came home after a long night of drinking and passed out on the bed. The next morning

I woke up covered in bruises. Emmy, that's my dead wife, she come into the bedroom as I was trying to figure out what the hell happened to me the night before. She looked at me and said, 'If you ever come around me or the children drunk again, I will beat the hell out of you. Then I'm gonna take the kids, move away, and you'll never see us again.'"

"That's called *tough love*," I joked as he continued warming up to me.

"I never knew for sure what happened that night until a couple of weeks before cancer ate up my Emmy. That's when she told me that she had smacked me several times with a rolling pin that night I come home drunk. She teared up when she told me, too," Robert said sadly. "But I told her, 'Honey, I'm glad you done it.' I wasn't too glad at the time, but my ways needed reforming.'"

I pictured my Mamaw sewing Papaw between two sheets and beating him senseless. I started thinking that maybe Mamaw wasn't crazy after all. Perhaps that whole generation believed you could beat the demon of addiction out of someone struggling. Then my next, selfish thought was *Thank God my Lydia didn't come from that generation!*

"I'm sorry your wife passed," I said. "How long has it been?"

"Sixteen years," Robert said quickly, as if he'd just been thinking about it. "My last drink was on April 17, 1965. I always figured I'd take up drinking again after she died. But that lesson Emmy pounded into me that night stuck."

"Good for you," I told him. "You haven't had a drink in, like, fifty years! Thanks for sharing your story."

"So, you a reformed drunk, too?" Robert stated as a question.

I gave him the short version of my story, ending with, "And that's why I care so much about helping others."

Before I told Robert the intervention plan, I gathered more background on his family.

"When my pa was only eight months old, his pa died in a cyclone when their town near blew off the map, and his ma raised him ever since. Later when he got married, he drank like a catfish, sucking up whatever scum he could find," Robert said. "That's about all I remember of him, 'cause I was only six when he died. Heck, I also remember the smell of booze and oil and cigarettes on him. He worked on cars, you see. In fact, he was driving a car he'd just worked on when he drove it off the road and hit a tree. Killed him. The police said he'd been drinking."

"So your pa, you, and Bobby all lost your fathers when you were very young," I said.

"Yeah, I guess none of us had what you'd call a father figure around much," Robert agreed.

While the dad death cycle was just an odd, sad coincidence, I knew that three generations of drinkers was not uncommon. Addiction is a family disease, often showing up in entire branches of family trees. *Robert's dad drank. Robert drank. And now Bobby drinks.*

Just from listening to Robert, I could tell he may be a big asset in the intervention. Or a huge liability. I sensed that if I offered to hold Bobby down while his granddad beat him, Robert would be more than happy to lend a hand.

I told Robert the plan for the next night. Then I gave him homework. I asked him to write a letter to Bobby about how his drinking was hurting others. I added that he could even include something about how alcohol had affected Robert's own life. Then I asked him to write what support he would offer Bobby in his recovery, and what he would no longer do for Bobby if he refused help.

Robert complained about the assignment, telling me again that he ought to "just take Bobby out back and knock some sense into him." But he agreed to drive over from Albertville, and he said he'd think about what to say.

Just as we said goodbye, another call beeped in. Switching over, I answered.

"This is Randy Grimes. How can I help?" I asked.

"You can tell me that you're going to make Bobby pay to fix my truck!" the voice replied. "This is Teddy. Wilma gave me your number. I know what you want to do, and that's fine. Just tell me that weasel will pay me back."

I glanced at the list: *Teddy: Bobby's brother-in-law, married to his sister, Allison. Sigh.* Even in moments like this, I really loved what I do.

CHAPTER SIX

RANDY'S STORY

"I knew I never wanted to date somebody who drank,
chewed, and cussed. And then I fell in love with a
man that did."

—Lydia Brady

I understood Teddy's obsession with getting his truck fixed. After all, I'd enjoyed an attachment to more than one car, including the Monte Carlo I drove to college.

Foreigner's "Hot Blooded" blared on the radio, rattling the back speakers enough to vibrate the rear window with each bass note.

Truth be told, before leaving for college, I'd never spent more than a week away from my family. That's because our family never took vacations. Any free time or "extra" money went into sports. Football creates great worship services, but its tithes are high.

The drive to Baylor took only about two and a half hours, but it felt like I was sliding into a new universe. Fortunately, I had my buddy Kent with me to keep me company. Just as we'd been teammates in high school, we looked forward to dominating on the Baylor Bears football team. And we looked forward to sharing a room.

Entering campus for the first time as an enrolled student, I had a kicking car, the love and support of family, my sister nearby should I get homesick—and freedom!

I felt like a kid visiting Disney World for the first time. My eyes got big, and each new sight stole my breath. Everything looked more majestic than when I'd toured months before. And huge. The thousand-acre campus seemed like it could swallow up four or five Tylers.

I parked in front of the athletes-only dorm, where Kent and I would live for the first two years. Since first-year athletes were required to show up two weeks before other students, and one week before other athletes, we already felt like we owned the place.

After carrying a load of stuff to the second floor, we opened our dorm room door to catch our first glimpse inside college life. First impression? *College smells a lot like reefer.*

Our room held three people, and while we banged around moving in, a huge guy sat up and blank-stared two pinhole, bloodshot eyes in our general direction. I didn't know who he was or how long he'd been there—maybe a week or an hour before. But it was apparently long enough to move in, get toasted, and pass out in bed.

What the heck have I gotten into? I thought. I'd spent the entire summer working like a dog and getting my body in peak shape, so it took me off guard to see a fellow athlete lying in bed, whacked out of his mind.

After the guy fell on his back and started snoring again, I looked around, absorbing my new home. For a room that would house three big guys, it seemed small. Fortunately, we had an adjacent study room with three desks, so we'd have our own space for schoolwork. We would also share an adjacent bathroom with the three guys in the next room: one sink, one shower, and one pot for the six of us.

After settling in, I headed over to the stadium to find Offensive Line Coach John O'Hara along with Tight End Coach Bill Lane, the man who'd recruited me. I also met the legendary Head Coach Grant Teaff. In football, the reason for having us all come so early was so we could learn the playbook inside and out, get acclimated to the campus, learn everybody's names and positions, and make sure that we could find the stadium in our sleep—a common state when heading to practice in the morning. The stadium was way off campus, so we would drive there twice a day.

On the first day, one coach told our group of freshmen something I took to heart: "You were recruited because you were some of the best high school athletes. But this isn't high school. Last year, you were at the top of your schools. But if you want to succeed at college ball, you gotta do three things," he shouted.

"Shut your mouths." He held up one finger. "Listen to your coaches." He nodded to the other coaches in the room, popping up another finger to join the first. "And learn from the better players." As he finished, a third finger appeared.

I would make those three points my operating system. I wanted to be the best I could; I had given football my all since fourth grade. Also, I feared failure and embarrassment. I vowed to never do anything that would make my coach-dad want to carry me over his shoulder again.

So I shut up, listened, and absorbed every minute detail I noticed. I studied everything, intending to strive for excellence.

The coaches gave us an itinerary for every practice and meeting. During those first couple of weeks, we never had a spare second to be homesick or worry about how we'd squeeze in a class or two once the academic year started.

True to the coach's words, practice at Baylor was nothing

like high school. Not that I knew from personal experience, but from the movies I'd seen, this seemed more like military boot camp. The coaches worked our butts off around the clock. We showed up at the stadium at 8:00 a.m. to get dressed and taped by 9:00 a.m. Then we'd meet for an hour about what we'd do at practice that morning. From 10:00 a.m.–11:45 a.m. we practiced in full pads, and with full contact. Then we'd shower, get dressed, eat lunch, and come back for another meeting at 2:00 p.m. By 3:00 p.m., we'd be back on the field for another hour or so. Then we'd hit the weight room for another hour before showering, getting dressed, eating, and attending a nightly meeting from 7:00 p.m.–9:00 p.m.

And I'll tell you something. By the end of the evening, no one even thought about horsing around or partying. We slept like the dead until the next morning, when we got up and did it all over again.

And I loved every minute of it.

Meals were my favorite time. Athletes ate together in our own dining hall, separated from other students. My sophomore year, the school would try to integrate the two dining halls. That was a failure. The athletes ate all the food.

"Food fight!" someone yelled during one of my first meals.

I heard the commotion, but I never looked up. Handfuls of mashed potatoes and chicken bones sailed through the air.

My teammates teased me later, because as food flew in all directions, splattering everyone in the dining hall, I kept my face in my food tray, shoveling in as much grub as my mouth and stomach could hold. Heck, if a little extra food landed on my shirt or tray, I just ate it.

Between burning so many calories and needing to be as big as possible to play my position, I never missed a meal. No, sir. Six square meals a day with plenty of snacks. As center, I knew my catechism: to make sure no one got to our quarterback. That meant getting—and staying—as big and strong as I could.

Freshman football orientation seemed more like boot camp, minus the skill to kill people with bare hands. Maim, potentially. But not outright kill. We played together, worked together, ate together. In a short time, this forced structure and conformity forged camaraderie, teamwork, and, ultimately, friendship.

My first three weeks at Baylor were all about football. After a while, I got stronger, upped my conditioning, and decided I could probably start having a little social life too.

A Tyler friend was having a party. I squeezed into my coolest, tightest-fitting, Bike-brand coaching shorts and a form-fitting T-shirt. I showed up at the party and stood in the kitchen, where I could eat as much as I wanted without having to walk to fill up my plate.

While taking a bite, I spotted this girl across the room. I did a subtle double-take. Well, I say subtle now, but what does an eighteen-year-old boy know of subtle?

I can't forget the moment I saw her. In the movies, when a man sees his dream woman, everything else blurs except for the woman. She becomes instantly backlit, and a faint, invisible breeze tousles her hair. Butterflies and bluebirds hover around her head while "Foxy Lady" plays somewhere in the distance.

"*Wow*," I thought as I swallowed hard. "*She is smoking hot.*"

Okay, so I'm no poet. But I knew a good thing when I saw one. And she looked *beyond* good.

This girl had this beach-sunned hair and amazing green eyes that sparkled even from a distance. I didn't know her ethnicity, but her complexion was so dark that I supposed she was an import from somewhere exotic.

As I started lumbering her way, I caught a glimpse of myself in a mirror on the wall. *Well, at least my Bike shorts look good*, I consoled myself, as I came up with a less direct approach.

I asked around and found out her name. *Lydia Brady.*

"Lydia," I repeated to myself. "What an exotic name. Lydia."

I couldn't satiate myself by saying it enough. There was just something about her...

I had no idea how to handle this situation or carry myself. So I stalked her. What I mean is, I watched her leave with a big group of people heading to the chapel. I just fell in line like I belonged, keeping my eyes on her the whole way.

If we spoke that night, I don't remember. I just kept trying to get close enough to hear her voice, which I just knew would sound like an angel.

Later, I found myself walking to Waco Hall. This time I wore jeans and boots. And that's the night I heard her voice. I was right! She had an angel's voice—and a Houston accent! My honey-to-be was a native Texan!

"You're Lydia, right?" I turned on my charm.

"Yeah, and you're Randy." She flashed the whitest teeth I'd ever seen, and blinked her stunning eyes, keeping eye contact for long enough to make my stomach drop. "We met a couple of nights ago at our friend's. And then we went to Waco Hall for orientation."

No, I almost corrected her. *You went to orientation. I just went along to stare at you.*

"Oh, that's right." I tried not to seem too eager.

"I like your boots," she said with a sideways smile. "I'm from Houston. Not many people wore cowboy boots in my high school."

I didn't know what to say, so I just stared and smiled. Clearly, I needed to work on my flirting. But she didn't seem to notice.

Playfully slapping my arm, she laughed, "You are SO funny!"

Again, she seemed unaware that I had no game. She just laughed.

"Hey, Lydia," I pressed further, "If you're not busy later, I was wondering if maybe I could take you out somewhere. Do you like pizza?"

"Oh, darn," she replied. "I wish I could. I...well, I'm going out with someone tonight. But can we do it another time?"

"Yeah, sure." My gut dropped, thinking she had another date, but I tried to hide my disappointment. "No problem. But hey, then you better give me your phone number so I can find you later!"

After writing down her number—and memorizing it before I even put it in my pocket—we said goodbye and went our separate ways.

I called her the next night, and we went out for pizza.

And we had our first kiss goodnight.

I had fallen hard for her, and I didn't want to get up.

CHAPTER SEVEN

THE INTERVENTION

*"First you take a drink, then the drink takes a
drink, then the drink takes you."*

—F. Scott Fitzgerald

December 18, 2018

"He would stop off for a couple of drinks on the way home a
couple of days a week, but he always seemed fine, not drunk or
anything," Bobby's wife, Julia, told me when she called me
back.

"When did that change? Did he start drinking more at some
point?" I asked.

"Yeah, he started drinking more after he rolled the four-
wheeler," Julia agreed. "He had two surgeries to repair the
tendon and did physical therapy for about a year, but it still
hurt. And he was given pain pills."

"Do you know what he was taking?" I wanted to know.

"His GP gave him Tylenol 3," Julia replied. "But that didn't
help. The surgeon refilled his one-month prescription about six

times," she told me. "When he ran out, the surgeon cut him off."

"Did he stop then?" I asked.

"No, he found another doctor, one I knew from the hospital. I didn't even know Bobby went to see him until I saw the new prescription in the bathroom. I'm a nurse, and I've seen my share of addicts. I started getting scared by how dependent Bobby was on these narcotics, so I asked his doctor to cut him off."

"So did he stop then?" I asked again, already anticipating the answer.

"Well, he was so angry when he found out I talked to his doctor that he didn't come home for two nights," Julia answered. "He stayed with his mom. When he came home, I could tell he was still mad. But he never said anything. I think he started drinking more after that," she added. "I don't know that for sure, but he was gone until later at night, not even getting home to put Anna to bed. And he always smelled like alcohol.

"At the time, I was thinking, *at least he's not still on narcotics!* About a month later, I went into his truck. The registration for his truck came, and I went to put it in his glove box. That's when I found a prescription bottle written by a doctor from out of town. And he had more pills in the bottle than printed on the label."

"Just one?" I followed up.

"I found just one bottle, if that's what you mean," she told me. "I flushed the pills down the toilet. A couple of hours later, Bobby came in screaming, 'Where the hell is my medicine?' For the first time, I got scared of him. Anna did, too. He screamed, 'Stay the f out of my business. You don't f'ing understand anything!'" Julia said, sounding rattled as she relived that fight.

"I'm sorry, Julia. That must have been scary," I said, speaking from a place of experience as I flashed back on my own life. Shifting back, I added. "To your knowledge, is he still taking prescription drugs?"

"I think so," she said heavily. "But I don't even ask anymore. I don't want him yelling and scaring Anna. So I just avoid talking about it."

"That's rough," I empathized, once again working to stay in the present as I thought of my own life.

"I thought he must be cheating on me, because the only night he stayed home was Sunday," Julia said at last. "He would leave in the morning, and he wouldn't come back home until after midnight. So one night, I went to the bar where Bobby hung out after work. I don't know what I planned to do."

"Was he there?" I wanted to know.

"His truck was parked near the door," Julia nodded. "So I went and tried to see into the bar," she said. "I couldn't see anything, so I just opened the door a bit and peeked. Bobby was drinking. Alone," she sighed. "I don't know if I felt relief or anger. If he'd been cheating on me, I would have left him. But he just sat there drinking while I'm at home night after night with our little baby after working long days. And instead of coming home to be with us, he'd rather drink alone in that bar," she said with pain.

"So what was the last straw for you?"

"There wasn't a last straw," she said with some anger. "I mean, there were too many straws to count. He lost job after job. He got a DUI and lost his license. He said he wanted to get his life together and reevaluate things. I so much wanted to believe him that I didn't pressure him to find a job immediately. I just let him walk Anna to and from school. But that didn't last. In just a few days, he ended up driving Anna to school—without a license—after drinking. My friend works at the kindergarten. She called me at work to say she smelled alcohol on Bobby's breath. And that was it." Julia started breaking down.

"I'm so mad," Julia wailed. "I asked him to leave about a month ago. From what I hear, he's getting worse. Allison told me he wrecked Teddy's truck. I'm so tired of waiting for the phone call that Bobby's dead."

"I know," I empathized. "It's scary."

"But I also love him. And I miss him, as crazy as it sounds. He's..." she blew her nose and tried to regain her composure. "He used to be so kind and caring. He couldn't wait to start a family," she sobbed again. "I've never seen him happier than when he was painting the baby's room and shopping for baby clothes with me. He even cried when Anna was born. But I don't see that side of him now. I just see him waiting to die," she finished with another sniffle. "And it doesn't seem like he even cares."

"Julia," I said softly, "I know how tough this has been on you. We'll get through this together. We'll do our best to get Bobby help, okay?"

"So what does he have now, two or three DUIs?" she asked, sounding desperate. "Randy, he's going to kill himself if he doesn't stop."

"Julia, let's both pray that God will do a work in Bobby and bring him back to the man he was," I said, meaning every word of it.

After saying goodbye, I grabbed my can of dip and walked to the balcony overlooking the crystal-clear water below. *Nasty habit,* I scolded myself as I placed a small pinch under my bottom lip against my gum.

Talking to Julia about Bobby triggered me. I knew her frustrations, and I shared them. But my feelings had almost nothing to do with Julia, Anna, or even Bobby. My feelings were rooted in my regret for how I'd spent years emotionally dead to my own family.

I spit into an empty cup. Looking over the balcony down at

the water eighteen stories below, I saw a large manatee mother and her calf slowly shuffling to warmer waters.

That's what a good parent does, I told myself. *A good parent stays with the children until they can take care of themselves. And I wish to God I had been that kind of parent.* My eyes teared up.

In the *Star Wars* series, Darth Sidious tells young Luke Skywalker that *fear and hate feed the dark side.* For those recovering from addiction, nothing threatens ongoing recovery as much as guilt and shame.

Guilt says, "I did something bad"; shame says, "I am bad."

I spit in the cup again, just as the two manatees swam out of sight.

I know those whispers of guilt that rise up in me are not God's voice. God doesn't want me to live in constant defeat. He wants me to live in perpetual victory. I can't deny my past, but God has forgiven me.

Most recovering addicts need to keep forgiving themselves. Once guilt kicks in, it triggers shame, the cold boot-heel across the throat. But that's not what God wants for us.

Growing up, we sang these lyrics in church:
Whiter than snow, yes, whiter than snow,
Now wash me, and I shall be whiter than snow.

I'm forgiven. When God sees me, the darkness of my sins doesn't make it into his vision. I've been forgiven through His blood that has washed me clean, and now I am *whiter than snow*.

I spit again, this time getting rid of the dip.

Closing the patio door, I sat back down in my chair to sip my very cold coffee.

"Okay," I said aloud. "Who's next on the list?"

CHAPTER EIGHT

RANDY'S STORY

"You want to associate with people who are the kind of person you'd like to be. You'll move in that direction. And the most important person by far in that respect is your spouse. Marry the right person."

—WARREN BUFFETT

Lydia and I became an item at Baylor, so much that I brought her to my sister's and brother-in-law's house. As much as Lydia seemed to like me, she absolutely *loved* Roxanne, and the two became like the sisters they'd always wanted but never had.

Lydia and I learned quite a bit about each other.

For example, I learned that she was the youngest child and only daughter of a Baptist preacher in Houston, Texas, Reverend John. A. Brady and his wife Yvonne, and she had two older brothers, Scott and Johnny.

Lydia learned that when I hung out with my teammates, I drank a bit and got obnoxious.

I found out that she loved dance, cheerleading, and staying active.

She found out that I chewed and cussed a bit. Did I mention she was a preacher's kid?! Yeah, she was a good Christian girl.

She also became aware that if I had money for five burritos at Taco Bell, I would eat them all without sharing anything except my onion breath with her.

I learned that Lydia didn't see herself being with someone like me.

And she learned that I didn't like being in a relationship, period.

So once we started dating seriously, I felt like I was drowning. I initiated a conversation.

"These chains are binding me!" I foolishly blurted out. From there, the conversation slid downhill. And that's when we went our separate ways. I clearly didn't know how to be a good boyfriend.

Then I saw her again.

Call it jealousy or maturity, but I knew I needed her back. Okay, it wasn't maturity. Lydia just had a special something. I missed her. She made me feel warm all over. I started to think I might be that exceptionally lucky, one-in-a-billion guy who meets his forever love and soulmate on his first date during the first week of college. So I *needed* her back.

In hindsight, what I called luck was God shoving open doors and putting me in the right place. I finally realized I'd have to be an idiot not to walk through.

Plus, her dormitory was named Ruth Collins. Ruth is Lydia's middle name; Collins is mine. Fate, right? So I needed to do something.

Anyway, I borrowed my buddy's motorcycle and sat on it in front of Ruth Collins dormitory, hoping to kickstart our relationship again if she saw me looking so awesome. I guess you could still call that stalking. I had one trick in my toolkit, so I kept pulling it out.

And then I saw her. I wore dark shades, so she couldn't see me seeing her. But, oh, I watched her, and then I watched her watch me.

She wore this amazing karate robe, a *gi* I learned it's called. She was on her way to self-defense class. And she completely stole my breath.

My plan worked. By February of our freshman year, we were back together—as God and fate would have it.

But there were still obstacles. At Baylor, guys couldn't be in the girls' rooms, and our curfew was like 11:00 p.m. It was strict back then.

I was busy all day with football and school, so for a while, people didn't even know we were dating. We just saw each other at night.

We'd meet between our dorms on a bridge and make out. Then we'd drive to the marina. I'd eat ten 75-cent burritos bought from a rickety little stand. I never offered Lydia any, and she never asked. If that's not love, what is? She seemed more and more like my dream girl.

But it was when we met each other's families that I knew for sure she was more than just an extremely hot date. Lydia got in with my family right away. She'd grown up as a cheerleader and the baby of the family with athlete brothers, so she fit right in with the Grimes lot.

My mom loved that Lydia was a preacher's daughter.

"That's the kind of girl who will stand by your side and keep you out of trouble," my mom said, wholeheartedly approving of my girl.

Lydia loved my mom and sister. And my dad *adored* Lydia. He treated her like his own daughter. When Lydia was home-sick, having my family around filled something in her. During games, Lydia would sit with my sister, mom, and dad—cheering and talking about every play. My mom loved Lydia's passion and sweetness; my dad did, too, but he also loved how

Lydia seemed to love football almost as much as he did. Dad and Lydia did the color commentary during each game, then we'd all head to my sister's house for a cookout.

And I loved Lydia's family—along with everything in her life. Lydia took me to Galveston and introduced me to the ocean for the first time—which became my favorite place.

The longer I knew her, the more I saw beyond her stunning physical beauty and realized she really had *the whole package*. Lydia had this warmth and kindness wrapped up in sweetness and the most outgoing personality I'd ever known. To borrow a line from Hollywood, I wanted to be a better person when I got around her.

Our freshman year turned into our sophomore year, with football, study hall, and Lydia making up most my waking hours.

Things were going well. But being the bullheaded guy I sometimes was, we got in another minor fight over something I can't even remember, and we broke up—again.

Two days later, we showed up at the same campus event. Lydia was talking to a group of guys. I swear she intentionally did this in front of my buddies and me. She threw a perfect smile and glance, before pirouetting to gossip with her sorority sisters. She acted like she didn't care that I was seething with desire—which might have looked a little like jealousy to the naked eye.

We started dating again the next day. I couldn't let that happen again, so this time I told myself it was for good. Which meant I needed to put a ring on it.

Going into my junior year, between working out to stay strong for football, I waited tables all summer at a country western steakhouse, saving every spare dollar to buy her a ring. Since I had a big appetite, I didn't have a lot of spare dollars.

I carefully planned the proposal. We went to South Padre Island with Lydia's family. When we arrived at the breathtaking beach, the setting was perfect, like the cheesy stuff in movies. The sun still hovered in the sky over the glistening water. It was the perfect beach to get down on one knee, take her hand, and ask if she would make me the happiest man in the world.

So we walked out onto the sand...

That's as far as I got. My stomach cramped in a crashing wave of indigestion from whatever I'd eaten on the way.

Delay of game, I thought wryly, holding my gut as we hobbled back to the car. My proposal would have to wait.

I felt much better the next morning, so I started looking for an opportunity to try proposing again. Lydia and I hung out with her parents around the pool. For months, all she could talk about was her brother's upcoming wedding. Since that topic came up so frequently, I decided to use it as springboard to talk about *our* future.

With my arms draped over Lydia's shoulders, I said softly, trying to sound as charming as possible: "Hey, what about us getting married next summer?"

Lydia smiled as if waiting for something more. So I added, *"I mean, will you marry me?"*

Okay, plan B had a lot less romance than my original plan. And my proposal may have sounded like something I'd accidentally blurted out, but it wasn't. I adored Lydia, to the point of knowing I'd cherish her forever.

My parents had spent two years with her and also knew she was good for me. While it's true that my mom loved almost anyone—especially if they liked Jesus, football, and me—my dad was harder to please. It was his opinion that really mattered most to me. I'd sweated for weeks trying to get up the nerve to talk to my dad to get his approval before proposing. I told him my desire and asked what he thought.

"Randy," he said sincerely, "Marrying Lydia is a no-brainer. She's absolutely perfect for you."

The day after I proposed to Lydia at the pool, the two of us sat down with her parents around the kitchen table. I'd already talked to her dad, but I wanted to make it more official.

"So Lydia and I were talking, and...well, what do you two think of us getting married?" I tried not to show any nerves.

"You're going to finish school," her dad answered—sternly but lovingly.

"Yes, sir," we both answered—me in my most polite Texan, my heart pounding just a bit.

They gave us their full approval.

I eventually bought the ring, after the engagement, with my dad chipping in for half of the diamond from Service Merchandise. If you're too young to remember Service Merchandise, it was the bomb. They were the leading catalog-showroom retailer at the time, putting out massive catalogs with things like fine jewelry, sporting goods, toys, and electronics. When I saw the ring pictured, I also pictured my future: our wedding day, our brilliant, beautiful kids, and our happily-ever-after.

We were engaged our entire junior year. Between classes, football, and wedding planning, the year flew by. And to be honest, football took up nearly every moment of my time, which left most of the wedding planning to Lydia.

Our wedding was on May 22, 1982, and it was a family affair. All our siblings were in the wedding. My dad was my best man. Lydia's mother and sister-in-law sang. Lydia's dad was a pastor, and one of her brothers was an associate pastor, so they both married us.

Since Princess Diana had gotten married the year before, Lydia had all the bridesmaids wear similar poufy lace tops with taffeta. Lydia's parents bought her dress—a beautiful lace, ruffed dress. She wore a big hat and veil. Lydia's grandmother sewed on all the sequins and pearls.

The day of the wedding, I wore a grey tux. Lydia gave me just one job that day: *show up!*

The wedding went off without a hitch. We didn't have much

of a budget since neither of our families had piles of money. But it was still a beautiful event. Both of our mothers cried, and both of our fathers slapped my back and said things like, "You take good care of her."

For the reception, Lydia's family dug deep into their savings to put on the best spread possible for their only daughter. We had a lovely cake, punch, fruit, and piles of pigs-in-a-blanket.

That's when my kind in-laws met my ravenous Baylor football buddies. Before Lydia's family got to the buffet table, my teammates hit the line, shoving plates of those little pigs-in-a-blanket into their mouths and pockets, hoarding them. By the time her family came through the buffet, nothing was left.

Video cameras were fairly new and expensive at the time, but we went all-out to hire a guy to shoot the entire event, carrying a big camera on his shoulder. The footage turned out grainy, but the memories were clear: *she was the most beautiful bride I'd ever seen, hands down.*

I'm glad I have those memories, because a couple years later, I accidentally taped an episode of *Miami Vice* over our wedding. I'm lucky Lydia stayed with me after that.

As nice as our wedding and reception were, I could not wait for the honeymoon. We started edging to the door, saying our grand goodbyes and offering everyone hugs. Jogging through a sea of thrown rice, we made it to the car. And that's when I learned that one of my friends had locked the keys into our getaway car.

Talk about awkward.

We slid a metal hanger through the window gasket, fiddling with that car door for thirty minutes before popping the lock! In the meantime, guests were so hot they were dropping like flies and going back inside. By the time I got in the car, I looked like I'd been swimming in my tux.

As an added bonus, my buddies had written, "RANDY IS

FAT" on my car, which permanently stained the paint. I'm still pissed about that. I was not fat!

For our honeymoon, we spent the first night in a fancy hotel, then went to a friend's house in Port Aransas where Lydia cooked her first meal—fish sticks! Then we drove to South Padre Island about eight hours away, where we spent a few nights.

On our way home, we had a flat tire. But I had married my dream girl, so nothing else mattered.

What could go wrong? I thought, climbing back into the car for the ride home with my beloved wife.

CHAPTER NINE

THE INTERVENTION

*"The weak can never forgive. Forgiveness is
the attribute of the strong."*

—GANDHI

December 19, 2018

The next afternoon after my phone calls, Lydia and I got to the
airport a couple of hours before our flight to Atlanta.

"So," I said at our gate. "Can I fill you in on the calls?"

"Please," she responded. "But tell me a couple of times,
since there are a lot of names."

"You'll do fine," I winked, pulling out my little notebook
and shaking it over my head. "This is my brain, and I'm willing
to share it with you."

During dinner the night before, I'd filled Lydia in about my
first three calls. Then I had to speak at a local meeting. By the
time I got home, Lydia had already turned in for the night.

"Okay, so I told you about Bobby's grandfather, Robert, his

brother-in-law, Teddy, and his wife, Julia," I said, flipping through a couple of pages.

"Okay, Bobby is the young man, right? And Wilma is his mother?" she asked to confirm. "And Robert's the one in recovery, or no?" Lydia asked.

"Well, he's not what I'd call 'in recovery,'" I said, adding air quotes. "He's from that school that says you just need to man up and quit, which is what he did after his wife beat the crap out of him with a rolling pin!"

"Just like your Mamaw and Papaw!" Lydia laughed.

"Yep. Robert wants to knock some sense into his grandson. Real sweet guy, though. He's gonna drive a couple of hours to meet us tonight."

"Teddy's the one whose upset about his wrecked truck?" Lydia asked.

"Yes," I responded. "Bobby borrowed and wrecked it pretty bad, I think. And he was driving without a license and with at least one DUI."

"Can he legally leave the state with court coming up?" Lydia asked.

"Well," I admired my wife's line of questioning. "I explained the situation to Travis, and he had someone reach out to the district attorney," I told her. Travis was a counselor I worked closely with at a treatment center. People would reach out to me for interventions, and Travis and a team of case managers would work behind the scenes to help lift roadblocks.

"So Bobby can come to Florida?" Lydia asked.

"Yes, which is a God thing," I nodded. "The DA will push the court date out if Bobby enters treatment, and if we keep the DA informed. But if Bobby doesn't get help, the DA will nail Bobby. He's tired of drunk drivers in his jurisdiction."

"Thank God," Lydia responded.

"He may very well go to jail either way," I added. "But we

have a small window to start recovery work before he faces any charges."

"Do you know if they are believers?"

"I think so," I answered, again admiring my wife's depth of questioning. "Wilma says they are all 'good Southern Baptists,' and they used to attend church together."

"Well, I'm glad they have a foundation of faith," she replied.

We sat for a moment in silence, reflecting on the parallels between our lives, Bobby's family, and all the others we had helped over the years.

"I think you'll relate to Julia," I added, squeezing her hand.

"She's broken over her husband's addiction, right?" Lydia wanted clarification.

"She's strong, but she's afraid of living like this much longer —alone with her child, while Bobby flounders. She's afraid his addiction might kill him."

Lydia looked me in the eyes—not to inject shame over my past, but to demonstrate her compassion for Julia. In a flash, gratitude struck me in the gut for where I was in this moment —*I'm here with my beloved wife, helping others who are stuck.*

"Then there's Allison, Bobby's sister," I said, returning to my notebook—which also served as our guidebook for this intervention. "She's close with Bobby's wife and daughter and sounds protective of them. She's also concerned about Wilma's safety. She's eager to help."

"Is Bobby close to his sister?"

"Yes," I responded. "As the big sister growing up, Allison watched over him. Apparently when they were kids, all her friends wanted to go out with Bobby since he was cute and an athlete. Sound familiar?" I winked.

"Yeah," my beautiful wife smiled.

"And there's one more person: Gary, a family friend. After Rusty died, he looked out for Bobby, taking him camping and stuff. He loves Bobby."

"Is he nurturing? It sounds like Bobby needs a nurturing man there, since he lost his dad," Lydia said, remembering the details I'd told her the night before. "I can't imagine losing my dad."

"Yes, Gary even hired Bobby. But he had to fire him, too. Drinking at work, or smelling like booze," I added. "Bobby's coworkers noticed it. Gary didn't want an entire workforce thinking it was okay."

We checked the board and saw our flight was delayed.

"Hungry?" Lydia asked, realizing we had an extra forty-five minutes.

"Have you ever known me to reject a meal?" I smiled as we headed towards the airport restaurant directory. While we ate the airport's version of "gourmet" pizza, we reviewed the plan.

"So we'll drive two hours from Atlanta to Cosa..." I began as Lydia interrupted me.

"I think it's Coosa," Lydia said, looking at what I'd written down in my notebook.

"Okay, Coosa," I corrected myself, grateful again for her sharp skills and ability to keep me on track. "Wilma thinks that Bobby will be out all night."

"How does she know?" Lydia asked.

"She told me he sleeps all day, gets up late, then heads to the bar at dinnertime most nights," I explained. "So she should have no problem slipping out to meet with us and plan the intervention without him noticing."

"Okay, good," Lydia said, nodding.

"We'll all meet at Allison's house to go over the plan," I continued. "And from there, you know the drill." I took a big swig of iced tea that had enough sugar to give an antelope diabetes.

After eating, we waited by the gate without saying much. Finally, once in the air, I leaned over to Lydia.

"I thought you were going to leave me," I whispered to her.

"What?" Lydia asked, her emerald-green eyes registering surprise.

"And I wouldn't blame you if you did."

"I never left you, Randy," Lydia said confused. "What do you mean?"

"I mean leave me for good, like walk out of my life," I told her.

"I would have if God would have let me." She saw the pain in my eyes. "I'm not trying to be hurt or hurt you," she added.

"I know," I said, having nothing else to say.

We sat in silence for a few minutes as I stared out the window. I thought about my love-hate relationship with these interventions. I loved helping others. And I liked to think that by sharing my experiences and offering help, maybe I could keep others from falling as far as I had. But it came with a price —as I was forced to recall my past.

"I'm sorry, honey," I said, looking over at her.

Without a word, she knew what I meant—slipping her hand in mine and holding on for the rest of the flight.

CHAPTER TEN

RANDY'S STORY

*"Pray for intestinal fortitude, work hard, and keep the faith.
Oh, and pray for good luck, you're gonna need it."*

—JERRY REED

As I settled into the flight, I drifted back to thinking about my beginning with Lydia—before my addiction.

After our wedding, our new life together took on two priorities: getting back into the flow at Baylor and setting up house.

Lydia spent the summer taking classes so she could finish early, and I started summer workouts. We found this little one-bedroom duplex. It's true what they say about being young, poor, and in love. We didn't have much, and we didn't need much. We had each other. Family shared some of their used furniture to get us started. Lydia's parents gave us their old bed, and my dad gave us his old recliner and TV. We found this lime green couch at the thrift store, which today would be called something classy like mid-century modern. We just called it *affordable*. Lydia's mother made curtains for us.

We were down to $25 in the bank. So we decided to invest

some of that bounty on love. We spent $20 on a Siamese cat we named Rufus and a rhinestone collar for him. I loved cats, and we needed to make a family. I figured if we could keep Rufus alive, maybe we could have children one day.

In a blink of an eye, school swung back into session, Lydia jumping into student teaching while I dove into football.

During my freshman year at Baylor, we'd gone to the Peach Bowl, beating Clemson in '79. The next year, we took the Southwest Conference, only to get crushed by Alabama in the Cotton Bowl.

My senior year, the team wasn't on fire, but I was. I played in the Blue-Grey game in Montgomery, Alabama—a college all-star game. In January, Lydia and I traveled overseas for the Japan Bowl, where we were treated like royalty.

While football had consumed my life since an early age, I never gave any serious thought to playing in the NFL. I mean, those guys were really good. So I set my sights on something more obtainable, being the best college athlete I could before teaching P.E. and coaching high school football.

But during my senior year at Baylor, that all changed when pro scouts started to come around, and I got stronger. I realized I might get drafted. I just had no idea where—or how high I'd go. I hardly had time to stop and think about what it all meant, which was great, because it kept my eyes on my next game.

The recruiters swarmed in during January, leading to the April draft. Baylor hosted "pro days" once or twice a week, where the recruiters came to watch us do drills. With so many college football players out there, it shocked me that the scouts wanted to take time to meet us in person.

They took notes on my deep snap—and watched me run and lift.

As strong as I'd become, I had some stuff to work on. Luckily, the track coach offered to help me get my 40-yard-dash time down. He gave me some great pointers on my start—stuff like *staying low* and *finishing through*—things I wouldn't have learned from a football coach.

More good luck? Or God shaping my life?

Weighing in at 260 pounds, my size made me very competitive on the college field. But to be an NFL center, I needed to get downright huge. A center could get only so far with strong leverage and steady hands and feet; size mattered.

So I did two things to put on weight: eat and get introduced to steroids.

Say the word steroids today, and people look at you like you're crazy. Athletes get asterisks next to their names when they break records using steroids. Steroids are bad news, and I won't defend them. But I will say that back in my college days, no one fussed about using them. In fact, most athletes took them. It wasn't until later in my pro days that they started testing and talking about the side effects. Before that, any athlete could get a script from a doctor and fill it at Kmart. The guy you were blocking against took them, so if you didn't, he would eat you alive.

When I went to the combines in Indianapolis and Seattle, I was ready.

The combines occur in three events attended by scouts from the whole league—and you go by invite only. They bring in 200–300 of the best college players in the country. I went to two of the three.

The combines included several drills that you'd perform in front of all the scouts. And they'd film everything. You know that song from The Police "Every Move You Make"? That was the combines. Talk about scrutiny. In addition to all the rigors of physical testing, we took an aptitude test to ensure we had the mental horses to play under pressure. Then they held meetings about what life was like transitioning from college into the pros. They even brought in current NFL players to talk about what life was like in the big league. I soaked it all in, with big ears and eyes to learn whatever I could.

My track training paid off. I ran really fast 40-yard times—4.7 seconds. I am forever grateful to my track coach, Clyde Hart, for dedicating his time to me.

"You're moving up, Randy," the scouts started telling me. "We like what we see."

This was happening so fast; it was like a dream. I couldn't quite sharpen my focus to understand what it all meant. What I did know is that I'd married the woman of my dreams, all of my scores for the combines were making me a serious contender for the NFL, and things seemed to be sliding into place. Life was good.

On draft day, Lydia and I sat at home all morning, staring at our dainty, retro-looking French telephone. Today, we have ESPN and televised drafts, but back then we had no idea what was going on behind the scenes.

"I think you're going to get a call," Lydia assured me. "You'll see."

"Can we talk about something else?" I asked, overwhelmed with anticipation.

"Should we talk about having kids?" Lydia suggested.

We chuckled at her attempt to change the subject. You know when you try not to think about water when you're thirsty? All you can think about is water. As much as we tried to talk about other things, we kept coming back to one thing: football.

Growing up, football meant playing under the big lights with a bunch of my best friends and gaining the approval of my dad. But the prospect of playing in the NFL meant something else: providing for my beloved wife.

For her part, Lydia didn't care what I did, as long as it made me happy. She knew I loved football, so if I did what I loved and got paid for it, bonus. She'd married me, never expecting

I'd be a pro player. Since she'd finished her degree, she'd
worked hard as a substitute teacher, and she was perfectly
content to keep working hard for the rest of her life—as long as
we were together.

"I'll do whatever I need to do, honey," Lydia said. "If that's
teach or be your football wife, I don't care. I'm just enjoying the
ride with you."

Finally, the phone uttered its dainty scream at us.

"Play it cool," I said to Lydia but meant for myself. "I don't
want to seem too eager."

But there was nothing cool about grabbing a French phone
quickly. After the first ring, adrenaline kicked in like I had just
stepped onto a field in front of thousands of fans. I snatched the
receiver.

"This is Randy Grimes," I said, wondering if whoever was
on the other end could hear my pulse in my voice.

"Randy, John McKay from the Tampa Bay Bucs," a raspy,
cigar-strained voice told me. "We just drafted you in the second
round. See you tomorrow."

"Okay," I said. "Thank..."

Click.

Twenty-two years of life came into fruition with those three
short sentences. Football went from my hobby to my passion to
my Texas religion—to the disbelief that someone-is-actually-
going-to-pay-me-to-do-what-I-love *career*.

I later learned I was the forty-fifth player taken, in the
second round of the 1983 NFL draft. Tampa didn't have a first-
round pick that year. They traded their first-round pick away
the year before, so I was their first pick. No pressure, right?
They were betting an awful lot on me.

After embracing Lydia and crying several tears of joy, I ran
through the house and headed outside—like I was running
through the tunnel to the football field. Once outside, I looked

up at the sky, expecting to see God appearing from the clouds wearing a foam #1 finger and proclaiming that I deserved this.

But I didn't see God. Nor was there all the hoopla there is today when someone gets drafted, with a two-day televised spectacle, green rooms, private jets, and endorsements. But as I gazed up at the blue sky—with a contrail streak from a jet overhead and a slight breeze on my face—I felt God's provision over me, basking me in His light.

CHAPTER ELEVEN

THE INTERVENTION

"There are no accidents; there is only some purpose
that we haven't yet understood."

—Deepak Chopra

December 19, 2018

About six hundred miles separate West Palm Beach, Florida, and Atlanta, Georgia. We left Florida under clear, sunny skies. In Atlanta, rain mixed with snow flurries made me glad we'd dressed like we were heading to Alaska. In a couple of hours, it felt like we'd gone from the tropics to the Arctic Circle.

After getting our bags and rental truck (I like to rent something my size), I reached out to Wilma. She told me that Bobby had already left for the evening. We started driving to Coosa.

The drive seemed longer than the ninety minutes predicted by the GPS. Part of the delay had to do with driving in unfamiliar surroundings. The rest had to do with the weather. Florida has its share of heavy downpours. They don't tend to last long, but they delay planes. In our case, we left Florida later than planned. Now in Georgia, guiding the car in the dark through relentless, blinding rain made me drive even more cautiously.

Pulling up to the house, we thought we must have the right place when we saw a wrecked truck on the gravel driveway. Only a dim, yellow light showed through the glass on the front door. While the other homes along the drive were festive with Christmas lights, this home sat stark in contrast. It's as if the cheer of the holiday completely skipped over it. Adding to the bleakness, the fence behind the home fell in disrepair, and the siding shed ribbons of peeling paint like a snake losing its skin.

"Okay, this is the place. Let's do this," I said.

"Wait," Lydia responded. "We can't do this alone."

Lydia and I held hands and bowed our heads before leaving the car. "Lord," I started. "We need your help, and so does this family. Please use us tonight to unite them in helping Bobby."

"Heavenly Father, give us the words to say," Lydia continued. "Work even now in Bobby's heart and bring him back to you."

"Amen," we said in unison.

I grabbed my phone and car keys. No matter how many times I'd done an intervention, it always felt like the first. I never knew what I'd get into. Even though I'd spoken to these folks over the phone and gathered many of the facts, interventions have too many variables to just assume you can walk in fully prepared.

"Okay, it's time," I told Lydia, opening my door and stepping into the blowing rain.

Lydia pulled the hood of her coat up over her head as the wind and rain pelted her.

We walked as quickly as we could—which with my bum knee, wasn't very fast—and got under the shelter of the porch. I used my hands to wipe off the water from my coat, so I wouldn't track too many puddles inside the house. Then I knocked, seeing no doorbell.

We waited.

Nothing happened. We heard no noise from inside the house, but then the pounding of the wind and rain would have blocked out nearly every sound but a jet engine landing on us.

Finally, the door opened, and a slight woman in a red sweater and blue jeans motioned us inside.

"You must be Randy." She peeked into my face before looking away. "And this is your wife," she asked as more of a statement.

"Yes," Lydia moved forward to hug Wilma. "I'm Lydia. So happy to meet you."

As Lydia reached out to hug the small woman, Wilma turned slightly to one side, making the hug awkward.

"Nice meeting both of you," Wilma said. "Well, come on in a minute." She motioned us into the kitchen, which sat at the middle of the home.

"It's a nice place you have," I said as we walked from the dark entrance into the slightly less dark kitchen. "It's very cozy and warm." I uttered the only two things I honestly felt as I looked around.

"You'll find out sooner or later," Wilma said with her back turned. "Bobby was in a bad mood when he left. I think he'd been drinking or something in his room, because he didn't look like hisself when he came out."

"Okay?" I turned that word into a question.

"Anyway, when he tried to get by me, he bumped into me and did this." Wilma turned to us for the first time, revealing swelling around her left eye.

"Let me get you some ice for that," Lydia said. Springing into action, she opened the freezer door and removed an ice tray. "Do you have a small plastic bag for some ice cubes?" she asked.

"They're in the drawer under the microwave," Wilma said without looking up.

Turning to me, Wilma seemed anxious to say more. "I know I said I wasn't sure that he had a drinking problem," she began. "But he does. I'm sure. I think it's getting worse. But *this* was an accident." She pointed to her face.

Lydia handed Wilma a small bag of ice wrapped in a kitchen towel. "Here. Put this on your eye for a minute," Lydia said like the nurturing mother she'd always been.

"Thank you," Wilma said absently, holding it to her face.

"He tried to pass between me and the Christmas tree," she continued. "And he knocked it over trying to avoid me. But once the tree fell, his shoulder or elbow caught my eye. He didn't mean it."

"He's not driving, is he?" I asked.

"No," Wilma said emphatically. "He wanted to take my car, but I told him 'No way'! A friend picked him up," she explained. "Anyway, I was still cleaning up the glass when you came. I had some old glass ornaments on the tree. Most of them broke now."

"Is that all cleaned up now?" I asked.

"I don't know," Wilma replied. "I was so ashamed that I didn't want to turn on all of the lights to see if I missed some pieces."

Lydia turned on the lights and picked up the broom and dustpan Wilma had propped against the wall. While she swept up all the little shards of glass, I straightened the tree and plugged in the string of bulbs. Within a few minutes, we had the room back in order.

"How is your eye feeling, Wilma?" Lydia asked sweetly once we all regrouped in the kitchen.

"It's fine," she responded as she lowered the bag of ice. "Cold."

Standing in brighter light, I could see few wrinkles on Wilma's face. She had kind but tired blue eyes and graying, shoulder-length brown hair framing her face. Had I seen her on the street, I might have guessed her age as closer to forty than the fifty-two years I knew her to be.

"Is there anything else we can help with before we meet the rest of the family?" I asked.

"No," Wilma shook her head. "You've already gone above and beyond. Let me grab my purse, and we can go."

Once we all got settled in our Ford, Wilma started speaking again.

"Go back the way you came, to the stop sign," she said from the back seat. "Then turn left. Allie and Teddy don't live far."

After I turned at the sign, Wilma continued.

"I don't want you to think bad about Bobby," she said with some sadness. "He's had a hard life when his dad left us and then died. Him bumping into me was just an accident. He's not a bad boy."

"I understand that, ma'am," I told her. "But no one gets into a car accident *on purpose*."

"What's that?" Wilma asked.

"Well," I explained, "When Bobby wrecked Teddy's truck, that was an accident, just like when he hit your eye. They weren't an *on purpose*. But accidents have consequences. He will have a lot of legal trouble for driving under the influence. And if you were to call the police about what happened tonight, he'd be arrested for assault."

"I know," Wilma protested. "But I paid his bail to get him out of jail. And I'm not going to call the police on my son...Turn right at the next road."

"We just want to get Bobby help, so he doesn't have more accidents, especially ones that seriously hurt someone," I assured her. "As long as he's drinking or taking pills, he puts himself in great risk."

As we passed several homes with bright, festive Christmas displays, my heart sank with a familiar feeling—knowing that Bobby's heart was too numbed to feel or notice any holiday spirit. *Addiction has him by the throat,* I thought while making the final turn before our destination.

CHAPTER TWELVE

RANDY'S STORY

*"Give me six hours to chop down a tree, and I will spend
the first four sharpening the axe."*

—Abraham Lincoln

Sometimes it's that place of being on top of the world that provides the biggest opportunity to fall.

When I got drafted into the NFL, Lydia and I weren't the only ones celebrating. When our families heard the news, you'd have thought they'd all been drafted, too. My dad even bought me my first sport coat. He wanted me to look nice for the media around Baylor and Tyler, who all wanted to cover the news of *the local boy who'd hit the big league.* While there wasn't the media hype of today, I did get what felt like a lot of attention at the time. Immediately after some local interviews, I flew to Tampa to check out the area and make everything official. They threw another media event for me there.

In no time, I started rookie mini-camp, where they brought all the new drafts and free agents. I got handed a playbook, which I studied like the Bible. I was determined to learn the system and all the people I'd need to know. I kept a close eye on those who'd been around the team for a while, so I could learn from the best. Luck and discipline had brought me this far, and I told myself that I would take full advantage of this opportunity and *be the most successful center Tampa Bay had ever seen.*

I was drafted in 1983; Tampa had made it to the playoffs in 1982. As far as I knew, I was joining a playoff team—in a seaside community. This was as good as it gets for a wannabe cowboy who'd first seen the ocean just a couple of years ago.

Shortly after that rookie camp, I flew back to Texas once more to pack up everything. Whatever didn't fit in our U-Haul, we stored in our parents' garage.

And then just like that, we headed to Florida where I would trade in my cowboy boots and denim for Tommy Bahamas shirts and pastel shorts.

A month after the draft, my good luck continued. Before relocating to Florida, Lydia had some news of her own for me.

"Hey, babe," she asked me over dinner. "Do you remember what I asked you when we were trying our best not to talk about the draft the day of the call?"

"Huh?" I asked between bites of Texas beef. "What did you ask me?"

"I asked you about having kids," she said.

I had a lot on my mind, so I wasn't firing on all cylinders at first. And ever since my first year in college, I had a way of shutting out all distractions while in front of my feed trough. But Lydia's words started to penetrate my thick skull, and my chewing slowed.

"What? Are you saying what I think you're saying!?" I tried to swallow and talk at the same time, while nearly choking in the process.

"Well, I don't know if it's a boy or girl," Lydia smiled. "But you're going to be a daddy!"

We laughed and cried together. *I mean, who has better luck than good ol' Randy Grimes?* I thought. I had a new job in a new state, doing what I've always loved. And on top of all of that joy, we were going to be parents.

The good news kept coming. Upon signing with the Bucs, they issued me a sizable signing bonus. They called it a loan, but I didn't have to pay it back. That bonus combined with my first-year salary gave me more money than I'd ever imagined. Overnight, I had more earning potential than I could comprehend.

We were so happy, I even let Lydia's dad talk me into buying a Peugeot 505 STi sedan. This cowboy and cowgirl would arrive on the Southeast coast driving a French car.

The downside of driving from Texas to Florida while Lydia was pregnant is that we had to stop every hour for a potty break. Even with the blazing July heat, I didn't mind, because we were living a wild dream.

We rented an apartment for a few months before buying a two-bedroom condo in part of Tampa where many players lived. Finally, we could afford new furniture for the first time, so we chose a bunch of rattan stuff. We figured since we lived near the beach, we should have a beach-themed home and furnishings.

Once Lydia set up the nursery, we were ready for our baby. Even the long, hard days of working out and practice couldn't knock the grin off my face.

I had started bulking up in college, but now I kicked it into overdrive. To satiate my unending appetite, Lydia cooked for me. Meat, potatoes, vegetables, desserts: it didn't matter what it was, if she could find a way to fry it, I found a way to eat it. I ate, and I played football.

Our training facility was called One Buc Place. Every day we lifted weights, spent time with coaches, and "did film"—which meant watching footage of plays, other teams, and critical games to know what we'd be facing the next season. This all led up to official training camp.

I felt the pressure of being the Bucs' first draft pick. They had just hired a new offensive line coach, Kim Helton, who came from University of Miami. The guy who played center for the Bucs, Steve Wilson, had no idea they would draft a center, so he was in shock. He could have been bitter and scared, but he turned into a close friend. Our two families eventually got close, and our kids played together all the time. Steve and I probably connected because we shared a mutual love of fishing. More good luck!

Actually, by this time, my belief in good luck started to wane. A string of minor miracles could not be labeled as simple luck. I believed God was watching over us, putting us where He wanted us. He was *blessing* us.

Training camp started around my birthday in late July. The Bucs were one of the first teams to report, which was ridiculous, because we were in one of the hottest places on the planet. In hindsight, I think playing in the torturous heat may have been part of the Bucs' plan to fuel our endurance.

We stayed at the hotel next door to One Buc Place called the Hall of Fame. But insiders called it the Hall of Shame, because it was so run down and shabby.

Bouncing between the hotel to One Buc Place, one day I stopped and looked around. Even though I was beat up, exhausted, and dehydrated, awe filled my heart. Big players I'd admired like Lee Roy Selmon and Dave Logan stood beside me. Doug Williams arrived for training camp before leaving to play for Washington. I walked behind Hugh Greene, the All-American linebacker out of Pitt. Next to Hugh walked Seann Farrell, a first-round pick out of Penn State. I got to stand next to men like Beasley Reece, who now serves as the director of the NFL alumni. And Mark Cotney. These were some of the greatest players in the NFL, many of whom had come from other teams.

I shook my head, so amazed that *Randy Grimes from Tyler, Texas,* stood amongst these football greats. In no way did I feel equal to these legends, but I went through the motions to fit in, pretending I didn't have to fight the urge to bow down to them and say, "I'm not worthy!"

Today, national media attention is huge and ever-present. That wasn't the case back in the early eighties, as I've said. But our local media kept covering me. They interviewed me, wrote articles about me, and filmed everything I did—capturing every word I said. I felt like I'd made it big. And I felt like I better make good on it and live up to the way they kept hyping me! No pressure, right?

My sister, Roxanne, wrote me a letter that started with "Dear Bubba." Steve Wilson, the center I befriended, saw it. Before long, all the team, media, and announcers called me "Bubba Grimes." I didn't mind, as it reinforced that I was part of a family.

The coaches didn't deviate from our training itinerary, and in my opinion, they didn't need to. I decided their plan was perfect. Our two daily practices were filmed. At team meetings, we watched the daily film before breaking off as an offensive line to see more specific footage. Several cameras were always rolling, filming different drills and angles. Then we'd go over plans and goals for the next day.

Besides practice and meetings, we lifted weights, saw the trainer, attended to any injuries, rested, and ate. Some days, we had scrimmages.

After all of this was done, we'd have up to an hour to run to a bar for a beer or go home and see family.

I didn't have much free time, but that suited me fine. I thrived on the structure. I wanted to be *the best*, which meant learning from the best. I became a sponge for picking up and copying what worked.

As I lay in my hotel bed one night, it began sinking in that football had become a real job, not just a sport. I must be prepared for whatever they wanted me to do, and it was becoming clear that their expectations were that I should be able to do *anything*.

Will I be up for anything? I fell asleep wondering, as I drifted in and out, dreaming of Lydia. She was smiling, and I was trying to get to her in a crowd. And the best part is that she was looking for me, too. I laughed a bit as I drifted off one last time to sleep for the night.

The next day, we hit practice hard all over again.

The Bucs were still considered a new franchise in the early eighties, having formed in 1976, the same year as Seattle. But even though they were new, having made it to the playoffs the season before, as I looked around the talent on the team, I was even more sure we were building a championship team.

After what seemed like years of training camp, the season finally started. Each day, I learned how to be a better NFL center. I couldn't wait to get in there and show them what I could do. While watching from the sidelines, I fought the urge to belt out a couple of lines from that Credence Clearwater Revival song: *"Put me in, Coach! I'm ready to play today!"*

But I knew how it worked. I would do my part to be ready when the time came. I was willing to pay my dues.

This is it, I told myself. *I've nearly arrived. Now all I have to do is keep working hard—and not screw it up.*

CHAPTER THIRTEEN

THE INTERVENTION

"It was a dark and stormy night..."

—Washington Irving

December 19, 2018

"Mom, what the hell did he do to you?" Allison asked when she saw Wilma's eye.

Allison and Wilma looked more like sisters instead of mother and daughter. Like her mom, Allison had blue eyes with chestnut hair, but her long legs made her look like a runner.

"Watch your language, please," Wilma scolded her daughter before minimizing her swollen eye. "And this is nothing. Bobby accidentally bumped into me when he left tonight."

"Are you serious?" Allison shouted. "Teddy, come look at what Bobby did to Mama!"

Teddy appeared from the next room with a beer in his right hand. Dressed in jeans, a T-shirt, and a thin fleece vest, Teddy looked like a lumberjack, complete with dark red hair, a scruffy beard, and light green eyes. I remembered that Teddy had a small construction company, and judging from the thickness of his arms and neck, he did a lot of heavy lifting.

"Whoa," he said when he saw Wilma. "Bobby did that?"

"It was an accident. He tried to walk between me and the Christmas tree, and he just bumped into me. He didn't hit me or nothing," Wilma said, her defenses rising.

"Hi," I interrupted. "I'm Randy, and this is my wife, Lydia."

While exchanging pleasantries, the bathroom door opened, and an older, heavily-bearded gentleman approached.

"I'm Robert." The man shook my hand with the strength of a linebacker.

"Hi, Robert," I said while our hands locked, introducing Lydia.

"What the hell happened to your eye?" Robert asked when he saw Wilma, nearly echoing Allison's question.

"Hi Daddy," Wilma said, sounding younger, as if she'd stepped back in time.

"Hey yourself," Robert said, as he gave his daughter a side hug. "Did Bobby do that?" he asked, nodding to the swelling on the side of her face.

Wilma again tried to explain that Bobby had bumped into her *by accident*. She sounded almost apologetic.

"I'll tell you what," Robert said emphatically. "I'm gonna have an accident all over that boy's head!"

"That's what I'm saying," Teddy agreed. "First, he's driving around drunk. Then he wrecks my truck. Now he's hitting Wilma? This shit has gotta stop."

Trying to interrupt the growing negativity, I asked, "Is Julia here?"

"No, she's on the way," Allison replied. "She called a few minutes before you got here saying she got a sitter and would head over soon."

Allison motioned us into the family room, while Teddy held up a finger for me to stay back.

When alone, he asked, "Hey, Randy. Does it bother you that I'm having a beer? I can put it away if it's a problem."

"Thank you, Teddy," I replied. "I have no problem with you having a beer. I do, though, have a problem with *me* having one."

"Okay, great," he said. "I'll finish it here in the kitchen and then join you."

As I sat on a big sectional next to my wife, Lydia spoke.

"You have such a lovely home, Allison," she said with her usual grace and sincerity. I admired how Lydia could always make people feel comfortable—which made it a lot easier to help families. "How long have you lived here?"

"Thank you," Allison answered. "We've been here about twelve years. You should have seen it when we first bought it. Teddy tore it down to the studs and rebuilt it himself."

"Wow," Lydia said, looking around. "He's talented. No one in my family would know where to even begin doing something like that."

"Excuse me," I interrupted Lydia with feigned offense. "I know how to tear things apart," I puffed out my chest and spread my arms wide to show my size. "The problem I have is putting them back together."

Everyone laughed. It felt good to relax for a moment before jumping into the night's serious work.

Soon, we heard a knock at the door, followed by a young woman's voice.

"Knock, knock," a woman said. "Anyone home?"

"Hey, girl," Teddy said kindly as he gave his sister-in-law, Julia, a hug. "Are you hanging in there all right?"

"Hey, Teddy," she said, hugging him back. "Yeah, I'm okay. I'll be a lot better if this all goes well, but God knows I'm kind of nervous about it all."

"Hi, I'm Randy," I said, as I stood and extended my hand.

When Julia turned towards me, a thick tangle of her wavy, light brown hair fell over half of her face. Ignoring my hand, she fell into my chest and gave me a long hug. She felt small and fragile in my arms. From her breathing, I could tell that she struggled to keep back tears.

"It'll be alright," I assured her.

"Thanks for being here," she said softly. "I feel like you're our last hope."

As we embraced, Lydia spoke.

"Oh, sweetie," she said to Julia. "I'm Lydia." My wife wrapped an arm around the small woman.

Without looking up, Julia released me and turned to hold Lydia with same desperation she'd clung to me.

The rest of the family started joining in the embrace.

"Aw, come here, Hon'," Wilma offered as she hugged Julia from behind. "I know this has been so hard on you and little Anna."

With the mention of her daughter's name, Julia let her tears flow. But when she turned towards Wilma and saw the bruising around Wilma's eye, her tears turned to sobs.

"It's okay, Baby," Wilma cooed. "This was *just an accident.* Everything is gonna get better from here. Okay?" Each time Wilma said "accident," she seemed to get more comfortable with the word; but I hoped she may also be realizing she shouldn't sugarcoat Bobby's behaviors too much.

Another rap sounded on the door. A lean, gray-haired man with a weathered face entered.

"Gary!" Allison said quickly. "Thank you for coming."

"It's been a while since I've seen you in town," Gary greeted Teddy after finishing his embrace with Allison. "You still driving that old Bronco?"

"No, I sold that a while back and got a new truck," Teddy answered as his face started to cloud over.

"Let's not talk about that now," Allison said. "Maybe we should get started," she suggested.

"That's a great idea," I seconded. I was grateful that someone besides me started to take charge of group. "This won't take long, I promise."

Once all the greetings were done, I found an open chair that faced the sectional sofa. Julia settled on the floor with her legs drawn up and a pillow in her arms. Lydia joined her on the floor and rubbed Julia's back for comfort.

For a fleeting moment, I wondered if this is what Jesus felt when he had a bunch of disciples gathered around him. But then I was quickly humbled, remembering that the Son of God taught others from His position of sinless perfection, while I could only try to guide others using the many personal mistakes I'd made.

Lord, may my past failures help this family tonight, I prayed silently to myself before getting started. The stakes were high; Bobby needed the same grace God had granted—many times before.

CHAPTER FOURTEEN

RANDY'S STORY

"That's gonna leave a mark."

—CHRIS FARLEY, *TOMMY BOY*

My family, like Bobby's, had been there to support me. Many of those times took place around football. They couldn't have been prouder of me than when I entered the NFL.

Once my first NFL season started officially, the Bucs' itinerary took us to Texas Stadium to play the Dallas Cowboys. Tyler people are Cowboy fans, but I'd never seen the Cowboys play live. Now, all my Tyler friends and family were driving in for the game.

The Bucs had a guy who played left guard. In this game, he was set to go against Randy White of the Cowboys, an all-pro with a huge resume.

Now, I couldn't prove this, but I'm pretty sure my teammate was scared to death to play against Randy White. I got confirmation on the day of the game when he had a mysterious "groin injury" during warm-ups.

"Grimes, you're left guard," I heard my coach yell. *This was what it meant to be ready for anything.* I was a center, not a guard. But this was time to step up and prove myself. And what better place to get my first start than in front of all my friends and family?

During warm-ups, I took a crash course on the plays. Yeah, I knew the playbook, but I'd learned it from the position of center, not left guard. I crammed. Eventually, I was ready...but scared. These were the Cowboys. As a lifelong Cowboys' fan, I had watched Randy White since high school. I'd cheered him on as he mowed down left guards like they were Girl Scouts. And in my NFL debut, I'd be going head-to-head with him.

As I entered the field, my fear of being killed by Randy got replaced by a new fear: I pictured myself running out on the field, tripping, and falling as my teammates crushed me on their way out. Fortunately, that fear didn't play out. Instead, I cruised through the tunnel towards the blue star at center field. Before stepping onto the field, I glanced up at the hole in the roof where God watched his Cowboys play. My whole family and a lot of my friends joined a sea of thousands roaring in the stands. I felt like I was watching on a screen, like it wasn't real, and someone would soon turn it off. But the footage kept rolling, and I had the ability to influence it.

Stepping out of the locker room tunnel into the sunlight where the stadium engulfed me, the scene hit me like a drug. *I was born for this, Baby!* My fear and excitement quickly formed into pure adrenaline as I geared up for the first play.

This was no college game. Guys in the pros were much faster, stronger, and more aggressive. These players had lots of experience—and they were smart.

I was there, on the field, with guys I considered legends. This was the day where I would earn my chops—transforming from a boy into a man.

But growth isn't always pleasant. Let's just say that Randy White tore me a new one that day. On my first start in the NFL, he hit me so hard that I saw stars and heard ringing in my ears. I'm not exaggerating. I felt like an old cartoon character that just had a piano fall on his head.

After that play, Randy put his hand down to help me up. It wouldn't be the only time he extended that courtesy, as he knocked me down time and time again.

We developed this little routine where Randy would knock me down, and I'd look up and say, "Thank you, sir," each time he helped me out. I extended my best Texas respect of "Thank you, sir" about twenty times that game.

"Quit calling me sir," he finally blurted out, laughing.

"Yes, sir," I blurted out, realizing I'd just embarrassed myself again. *Rookie error.*

I think I may have been bigger than Randy. But clearly, NFL success isn't just about size. It's about experience and aggression—and comfort in navigating the field.

Plus, experienced guys can pick up on fear. They smell it.

Still, I think Randy knew I was trying as hard as I could, and he respected that. He knew I was a rookie. He probably knew that it was my first start, and I wasn't even a guard.

Of course, that didn't stop him from tearing me a new one, I thought.

The Cowboys won that day, but I felt like the victor just getting to play against them. Afterwards I met with all my family. Even my cousins had come in to see the game. Lydia was beaming, starting to show her pregnancy. *We've arrived,* I thought.

It turned out that day would be memorable not just for its glory as my first NFL game. My moment of shame playing against Randy White also would live on—visibly...

The next year, the Bucs went to the Hall of Fame game at the beginning of the season. We exited the bus in Canton, Ohio, to tour the Pro Football Hall of Fame. This field trip was meant to inspire us to new heights, I'm sure.

Every year, sports writers and photographers would submit their pictures from the year before; the best picture would hang there for an entire year. As I walked in line with my teammates, feeling a little like a big shot, I rounded the corner to a room with a huge 10-by-10-foot mural. As my eyes locked on the photo, I froze.

My teammates, on the other hand, exploded with laughter.

In the photo, Randy White was reaching over me to get his massive hands onto our quarterback, who he was pulling down. As White stretched around me, he was having his way with me like I was a ragdoll. My face was all twisted and distorted, my helmet hung sideways across my head, and one of my ragged eyes managed to peer out from the ear hole.

That picture hung in the Hall of Fame all year. Yeah, God knew how to humble me. And it wouldn't be the last time.

CHAPTER FIFTEEN

THE INTERVENTION

"The act of writing itself is like an act of love. There is contact. There is exchange too. We no longer know whether the words come out of the ink onto the page, or whether they emerge from the page itself where they were sleeping, the ink merely giving them color."

—GEORGES RODENBACH

December 19, 2018

While Bobby's family settled in, I pulled out my notebook, mentally checking off the list those present.

"When I talked to you all on the phone, it sounded like none of you have been part of an intervention before. Is that right?" I asked.

Heads shook across the room.

"Maybe you've seen a TV show about doing an intervention?" I continued.

Again, the room filled with shaking heads.

Finally, Teddy spoke up.

"I remember an episode on *Seinfeld* about an intervention," Teddy shrugged. "But I don't guess that counts."

A few people laughed, including me.

"No, that doesn't count," I laughed. "But it got a couple of things right. Like having the right people show up. Looking around this room, I'd say we got the right people. Every one of you has been affected by Bobby's substance abuse."

The group wore a collective of grim faces and nods.

"The purpose of this intervention is to confront Bobby about how his substance abuse is affecting all of you. And then we will ask him to accept help by getting into treatment," I shared.

"And I have some really good news," I continued. "First, Bobby is still on Julia's insurance. My boss did some checking, and Bobby's treatment will cost nothing or very little out of pocket. Second, y'all know that Bobby is facing criminal charges for the recent DUI. But the district attorney is willing to push out Bobby's court date if he goes to treatment. I've been doing this a long time, and I can tell you that's rare. So," I smiled, "Bobby has two good reasons to go into treatment right now instead of waiting."

"Give me ten minutes with that boy, and he'll be begging to go to treatment," Robert said dryly.

"I appreciate your enthusiasm in helping your grandson, Robert," I responded. "But in my experience, the best way to nudge someone is to have every person share something personal about how the disease is causing problems, instead of just having one person give a great big shove."

"I'm jes' saying he needs to be told how it's going to be instead of all that namby-pamby talk of feelings and disease," Robert continued.

"Daddy, please," Wilma said in a tone that somehow straddled deference and impatience.

Robert looked away, but he stopped talking.

"Did you all write the letters I asked you to write Bobby?" I asked, shifting the focus back to what was next. "I want each of you to take your time and write a letter to Bobby tonight to read to him in the morning."

A few people held up their letters, and a few more just nodded. Instead of answering, Bobby's grandpa Robert tilted his hand from side to side.

"What does that mean, Robert?" I asked, mimicking his hand motion.

"It means I thought about what I'm going to say," he said, then looked down. "I don't need to write it down."

"Okay, Robert, it's important to make sure that what you say is encouraging and..." I started.

"I know what I'm doing," he cut me off. "Do you really want me to go on and on about how I can't hardly read my own writing even with my glasses on?"

"No, you're fine, Robert," I acquiesced. "I trust you, okay. You got this."

"Wait, you want us to *read* him our letters? Isn't that more awkward than just talking to him? I mean, he's my brother. Writing a letter and reading it to him sounds awkward," Allison asked.

"That's a great question," I told her sincerely. "We'll all be nervous tomorrow. When we get nervous, we leave stuff out, or just respond emotionally. Writing it ahead of time helps you gather your thoughts while calm."

"The second reason I want you to write down your thoughts is that I want you to start by telling Bobby the things you love about him. Trust me, it's hard to keep a positive focus if the person you're talking to interrupts or tries to leave the room," I continued.

"Finally, I'll admit that you're right about it being awkward. I mean how many of us have ever written a letter and then read it to a person? None, right? When you pull out a letter and start reading it, Bobby will understand very quickly that this isn't just another lecture. It's formal. It allows you to stay a little more detached, because you have a script," I concluded.

"Okay, that makes sense," Allison conceded.

"Good," I answered. "So tonight, finish your letters if you haven't already. And start by telling him why you love him and what you miss about the old Bobby, the Bobby you used to know before his addiction took hold of him.

"For example, Julia," I said as she looked up. "Remind him about when you first met and what you felt. Remind him of your first kiss or how happy you both were when things were going well. Talk about Anna. Heck, you can even speak for her. Tell Bobby about what Anna loves about him, and remind him of all of the daddy-daughter times they had together."

"Wilma and Allison," I shifted my focus to the two of them sitting side-by-side on the couch, "Bring up the good times. Maybe it was a special vacation or a memorable holiday you all shared. Try to get Bobby to think back to before alcohol or drugs. Tell him what you appreciate about him."

"Like the good old days before I ever let him drive my truck," Teddy said sarcastically.

I nodded. "Not all memories are sunshine and roses. So once you remind him of how much you care about him, be brutally honest about how he's disappointed you. So Teddy, yeah, he wrecked your truck. He left you without a way to get to work. Tell him that."

Wilma shook her head. "I'm afraid that if he feels beat up, he'll take off. So why don't we just tell him we love him and want him to get help?"

"I know it's not easy," I agreed. "But when you're active in addiction, you don't think about anyone but yourself. He needs to know how he's hurt others."

"He's right," Lydia added. "And don't worry about hurting his feelings. If you do it right, you probably will hurt his feelings," she said, emphasizing the word *hurt*. "But you're doing it to help him and maybe even save his life."

"That's right. Tell him that you're tired of him hurting you, even if it's accidental." I turned to Wilma.

"And Momma, tell him that you're tired of him stealing from you," Allison said, catching Wilma's eye.

"He's stealing from you?" Robert asked at the same time Julia asked, "Wait. What?"

"It's okay," Wilma said. "The important thing is we're gonna help him. Stuff can be replaced, but I just want my boy back."

"Any questions about the letters you'll write?" I asked.

Every person in the room nodded except for Robert, who had taken out a pocketknife to pick something out from one of his fingernails.

"Good," I continued. "So when we start the intervention at Wilma's house, I'll ask you, Wilma, to tell Bobby that you've been worried about him, so you called me to see if I could help."

CHAPTER SIXTEEN

RANDY'S STORY

*"With all these forks in the roads of our path, why do so
many choose to take the knife?"*

—Anthony Liccione

In March during my first year in the NFL, our firstborn child
arrived, a precious girl we named Emily. With the arrival of this
little treasure, I took even greater focus on providing for my
family, doing everything I could to learn the ropes and be at the
top of my game.

The next year, we bought a house in Texas and kept the
condo in Florida. I'd shuffle between Florida and Texas, especially in the off-season, which was dedicated to eating, lifting,
and staying strong.

Whereas our first house was a little love nest for us newly-
weds, the house we got in Texas had everything and meant the
world to Lydia. It was a beautiful place for our family to gather,
grow, and play together.

That year, I opened a small gym with big weights in a Texas
strip mall. I went into business with Lydia's brother, Scott

Brady, who ran the business year-round in addition to working his full-time job. As a bonus, I had a place to hang out and stay strong off season.

During the football season, Lydia got involved with the football wives—doing fashion shows, charity events, and kids' playdates. Back then, the NFL was like a large, happy family. There was no cattiness or *Real Housewives* type behavior that you might expect when big money and personalities get together. In the early eighties, most football players considered themselves blessed to play a game they loved, just like I did. Anything that came with it was an added bonus.

It's fair to say that the Bucs treated us well—and we fit in. Fitting in is critical to any athlete intending to stay in the game. The best way to fit in with a football team is to stay in top shape during the off season, follow the playbook on the field, and manage injuries so they don't keep you on the bench.

The first two things are easier to control than that last one. Injuries happen. You play any full-contact sport, and you'll get hurt. Getting hurt is one thing, but facing a season or career-ending injury is another. I made it through the first season in my NFL career without an injury. But it caught up with me. In 1986, I ripped up my shoulder and needed surgery. That went well, and I was quickly back to playing.

Knowing that a serious injury or long recovery period can end a career, I determined not to let that happen to me. I tried to lay low and manage my pain. My family's livelihood depended on it.

I soon learned that managing my pain meant knowing how to medicate. This was just part of being an athlete, or so we all thought at the time. Players had no problem finding and using pain medication.

The FBI and DEA did huge presentations to all of us players each year to warn us about the dangers of street drugs, gambling, and people who would take advantage of our status.

Ironically, prescription drugs were never mentioned as a problem.

But they were offered as a solution.

After home games, trainers would stand at the locker room door with a cart and hand us a bag with two beers and two pills as we walked out. For pain, of course, and to help us get some rest.

I never took the beers after those home games. Lydia was always outside waiting for me. We never had beer in the house, and I wasn't about to disappoint her.

But I did take the pills. After all, they were prescribed as medicine to help get me back on the field.

After away games, I didn't have to worry about carrying beer out to the car or having Lydia smell it on my breath. There would be plenty of time to drink and medicate on the plane. So my routine was different.

When I played away from home, the bus would drive to the airport and head straight onto the runway, where we would board. We didn't have designated seats, but we learned where we could play dominoes together, where the quarterbacks sat, and where the linemen grouped. The coaches always sat up front, so we left those seats open. We chartered United, so we got to know our regular flight crew and learned the routine, settling in quickly.

As soon as we plopped our big, beat-up bodies in those plane seats, prescription meds and alcohol flowed. The crew pushed a cart down the aisle, loaded with beers. Following the crew, our trainer walked the aisle with a little bottle of pills, pouring them freely into our eager, beat-up hands.

"Want one?" he'd ask, holding up the bottle, not even telling us what they were. If we wanted to relax and maybe even sleep, we nodded yes. I learned they were called Halcion, which is like the granddaddy of Xanax—a lot more potent but shorter-acting.

"Got any pain?" he'd asked after he finished passing out the Halcion.

One time I hurt like hell, and I nodded my head. The trainer hustled back up front and grabbed another bottle, which held Percocet or Vicodin. He returned and poured a couple into my hands.

All we have to do is ask for it. I learned that real quick.

As I said, there was a purpose to their prescriptions. They wanted us to sleep instead of getting rowdy on the plane. And they wanted us not to hurt, so we could rest up and get back for the next game.

Back then, all we had for pain was whirlpool, ice, stim, ultrasound—and pills. Today the NFL has more innovative ways to deal with chronic pain—and more accountability in prescribing narcotics and benzos. But even guys I've talked to now—one, two, or three years out of the league—they never had any problem getting what they needed. All they had to do was ask. Maybe it wasn't handed to them as they walked out the door like it was us, but it was available.

When my career started, I asked for the pills, because I wanted to sleep. I didn't think twice about it. They were sanctioned by our team doctors, trainers, and coaches. After each game, we were all beat up and tattered, had just played our hearts out, and now it came time to relax. *I can't relax when adrenaline is still coursing through my blood and I ache from head to toe,* I thought. *So why not take a couple?*

About half of us took those pills, without suspecting they'd present any problem down the road.

Once we landed back in Tampa, many guys teetered off the plane—some of them not even knowing where they were—before they drove home. I did the same thing. And once I got home, I'd take another pill. By the time I woke up, my body felt rested, my head seemed clearer, and I was just fine.

All in a day's work, I told myself.

Or at least that's how it was for many years—until I was no longer fine.

As the years progressed, the pills handed to me by my team's medical personnel stopped taking the edge off. I'd take whatever they gave me, but I still had sleeplessness and pain. So I began my quest to get more.

To hone my role as NFL center, I'd mastered observing others who'd done it longer or better than me. I did the same to learn how to get more pills.

One plane ride home, I turned to my teammate on the left.

"Hey, you gonna take your pills?" I asked.

"Nah," he answered, "I'm good."

"Do me a favor then," I said. "Accept them when he comes by, and give them to me."

Then I turned to the guy on my right and had the same conversation.

Next thing I knew, I held six Halcion in my big, sweaty palm. I would swallow half my stash and tuck a few away in my bag until the next day when I could get more from the trainer.

Then I learned that I didn't need the trainer to act as my middleman. I could get them myself. Every player knew where the drug safe was. We also knew that the combination was the jersey numbers from three specific players, which made it easier to remember after a few knocks to the head. So while no one officially told us that we could grab what we wanted, it was an unspoken understanding. I assumed other teams operated similarly.

Still, I didn't want to be seen as that guy raiding the safe, so over time I talked to more teammates on the flights home so I could grab their pills. Just like I'd learned the game of football, my pursuit of scoring extra pills to take home became an extension of my game.

In 1988, I found myself at home on a day with no game, and I was wide awake. I'd pop a few Halcion, not really thinking about it other than the inconvenience of having to make sure I had enough. I'd wash it down with an opioid or two when I had them available.

If at any time my side game negatively affected my play, I would have stopped taking those pills. Or, if I could no longer play through the pain, I would have been cut. But neither became problems for me. In fact, that year was my best in the NFL.

On the outside, I was the top center I could be. The Tampa Bay Buccaneers awarded me *Player of the Year*, an honor I could never even have dreamed about a few short years earlier. I was a Pro Bowl alternate more than once. People in Tampa knew me, and I couldn't go out in public without people stopping me on the streets. I was on TV commercials. But one of my greatest honors became eating for free at the food court during my whole career at Tampa (something I never took for granted), because it was called Tampa Bay *Center*.

Our family was thriving, too. Lydia and I brought home a son, our miracle boy, August 2, 1988. We named him Brady.

Life was beyond good.

Probably boosted by my local fame and popularity, I found a couple of doctors in the off season who made sure I never ran out of Halcion. I even had a couple of pharmacies that would mail it to me when I traveled outside of Tampa.

For the rest of my playing days, I stayed on heavy doses of Halcion and pain meds. At some point, though, I started to miss blocks of time, even on the gridiron. I'd wake up on the couch after a game—bruised, scratched, dehydrated, with my fingernails torn—and with no memory of having just played. The first time it happened, it scared the crap out of me. But the next day as the team reviewed the films of the game, I saw that I'd played really well.

So what if I don't remember the game? I convinced myself. *Even on autopilot, I play like a warrior.*

What my family didn't know is just how far my side game started to reach. I started to take pills during the day and *before* games. When I slept, my family just thought I was exhausted from playing my heart out in the heat. Lydia was so busy raising our kids—and she was a great mom—that she did whatever she could to support me. She had no reason to be suspicious or concerned, because she knew how motivated I was to play and provide for our family.

By 1990, I kept racking up new injuries, but my successes grew too. Besides the fans, I became the most stable thing about the Tampa Bay Buccaneers, as we had a revolving door of coaches and players. Our fans and my teammates came to depend on *Randy Grimes at center.*

I played well, paid the bills—and passed out at home. When I was awake, I spent time with Lydia, Emily, and Brady. I had the perfect life, and no one could question that fact. I didn't stagger. I didn't get DUIs. *I can handle it*, I thought.

But unknown to my family or fans, I was slipping *off center* —into another reality that would threaten to steal everything I cherished and lived for.

CHAPTER SEVENTEEN

THE INTERVENTION

"A family is a risky venture, because the greater the love, the greater the loss....That's the trade-off. But I'll take it all."

—BRAD PITT

December 19, 2018

"He'll get real mad," Wilma spoke to no one in particular, once I laid out our plan for the next day.

"That's okay," I assured. "I'm used to people being mad at me. Once you introduce me, I'll tell him that everyone here cares so much about him that they've taken the time to write him a letter to read to him."

Wilma bit her lower lip.

"He'll try to leave," she said. Teddy and Allison nodded their heads in agreement.

"He might," I nodded. "But I'm pretty good at helping people decide to stay put."

"Headlock," Robert said under his breath.

"Okay, I know that this will sound crazy, but next I want to talk about where I'd like people to sit and the order I'd like you to read your letters," I told them.

I spent the next several minutes assigning seats and the speaking order.

When I got to Robert, I said, "Okay, Robert, tomorrow morning I'd like you to sit..."

"Yeah, I see where this is going," he interrupted. "You want me to sit outside in my truck," he deadpanned.

We all laughed, which was needed to break the tension.

"Yes," I laughed. "You can sit outside in your truck. Or you could," I smiled, "sit in the recliner I spied earlier at Wilma's house. It's next to the couch, but it's still very close."

After everyone knew where they'd be in the morning, I asked people to take their seats in order, as if this were a dress rehearsal. I placed my backpack on the couch to represent Bobby's place.

"Look around, okay?" I suggested. "Start picturing yourself reading to Bobby." I pointed to my backpack. "We'll be close together. That's on purpose. Any questions?"

"Good. Now Julia will be the last to read," I said. "When she finishes, I'll tell him that I can get him to a treatment center before the day is over. I'll say more, but that's the gist."

Silence hung in the air for a few moments. Then Wilma asked what others were probably thinking.

"What if he won't go?"

"When I talked with you all on the phone, I asked you to come tonight with two things: your letter to Bobby, and what you plan to change if Bobby refuses to go to treatment. Right?" I asked rhetorically.

In some interventions I'd done, the family was so angry from putting up with the shenanigans that their list took on a flavor of cruel and unusual punishment. Other times, like with families in denial or those who had enabled the substance abuser for years, people froze up, not wanting to make what would sound like empty threats.

"Can you give me an example?" Wilma asked.

"He's become physically abusive to you, Wilma," I said. "As a parent, I know this is hard. But for your list, consider letting him know that he won't live with you anymore. And that if he ever hurts you again, you'll call the police and press charges."

Wilma let out a long sigh.

"I can't write your lists for you," I told everyone. "You must decide what you'll do differently. You're doing this to let Bobby know that he can't continue, and to set your own boundaries. You're making his decision easier, because you're taking away his options to keep hurting you."

"Can't you just tell him that if he doesn't go to treatment, he's going to jail?" Allison suggested. "Isn't that what the district attorney said?"

"Yes," I agreed. "That's true. And I want to hold that one as a last resort. After you all say what you'll personally do if he doesn't get help, I can let him know that it's treatment or jail. But I don't want to start with that, because I consider that the 'nuclear option.' Once that gets thrown out, Bobby might feel like he's got nothing to live for and nothing to lose at the same time."

"Does this work? Do most people you've worked with go to treatment?" Julia asked, speaking up for the first time.

"It does, and they do," Lydia said with enthusiasm before I could respond. Lydia was especially passionate about participating in interventions, realizing that it was an option she never knew she had until it was too late.

Many interventions fail, usually because of poor planning, inviting the wrong people, or not having a treatment center lined up once the person is ready for help. That's why I go in with a playbook like I had in football. I get to know those on the intervention team, sometimes asking individuals to not attend if I sense they may do more harm than good. And I have a strong support team, and my wife who is so naturally kind and nurturing that people just love her. Finally, I have a strong back-office team to make flight arrangements, secure treatment centers, and make sure that the person can get help immediately.

"Here's what I can tell you," I said, leaning forward. "*If nothing changes, nothing changes.*" Then I added one more thing. "I've never worked with a person who refused to go to treatment after an intervention."

I didn't mention that getting people to walk through the door of treatment was the easy part. Getting them to apply what they learned was more of a lifelong process.

I felt the energy change in the room. What had started as an evening of trepidation had finally swung into the direction of hopeful anticipation.

Let's do this, I told myself, ready for the big event the next day.

CHAPTER EIGHTEEN

RANDY'S STORY

*"It's not that I've been invited to the hole I'm standing in.
It's that I accepted the invitation."*

—CRAIG D. LOUNSBROUGH

By 1990, a few of us on the Bucs started working together to hoard extra pills. We weren't junkies, but none of us could sleep without them. So we hit up more teammates to collect their pills after each game. At one point, I collected thirty Halcions on the plane. I'd split them up with two other guys and take my cut home.

Even with ten pills, I didn't have enough to fall asleep. Sleep became my pain reliever. Using Halcion to *numb my pain* seemed totally legitimate as a pro athlete. After all, I couldn't do the job the Bucs paid me to do if I couldn't function.

In August of 1991, I needed surgery to fix a triceps tendon I'd torn during training camp. I decided to stop the Halcion cold turkey before the surgery. It wasn't easy, but I didn't want to risk dying under the knife on the table.

Right after the procedure, I had a seizure.

"You've got a seizure disorder," a doctor diagnosed. Lydia was worried sick about me. I had brain scans, and they put me on Dilantin.

While I recuperated from surgery, I couldn't play. While it killed me to be out of the game, it gave me the rare opportunity to spend Labor Day in Texas. God had a hand on me, because that break allowed me to see my dad.

In the mid-1980s, Dad was diagnosed with cancer, so he'd been battling this disease for five years. His body bore the marks from needles full of chemo, leaving him covered in burns where they'd been inserted. My larger-than-life, strong dad was withering away before my eyes, reduced to skin and bones.

But when I looked at him from his bedside, all I could see was *Dad*. My love for him blurred any weakness in his body.

Dad never missed my games. From fourth grade, he'd watch from the sidelines or on the screen. After every game, our ritual was to recap the game together. He'd give me his honest opinion of how I'd played and anything I could do to improve.

Joining the NFL didn't change anything. I'd always wait for Dad's call, aiming to hear, "Well played, Son." His reinforcement meant the world to me.

He was my biggest fan—and my greatest coach.

To help Dad cope with his pain, his doctor gave him sample medications— Dilaudid. I was no stranger to opiates, but I wondered if his might be better. When I sat with him one night, he had thee sample pills next to his bed. I slipped two into my pocket. I figured it was okay, as long as I left one for him to sample.

I later learned just how much pain my action had put Dad through, and how much guilt I would suffer because of it. As Dad's condition worsened, he required more and more pain medicine. In excruciating pain, Dad asked Mom to bring him his painkillers. They were all gone, because I had taken them to feed my insatiable compulsion.

I saw Dad waste away, but I also saw him fight. He dragged himself into the office every day, deathly sick, just to get one day closer to qualifying for full retirement benefits. In his heart, Dad knew the retirement money would be for Mom, and this was his last great act of love for her. Somehow, I told myself they'd both enjoy it one day—once he beat this disease.

Each night, Mom rubbed his feet, trying to boost his circulation and warm his thin frame. I stayed by his side, helpless, still believing he'd win this fight.

I wasn't ready when he gasped one final time and let out a long, ragged breath before exchanging life on earth for an eternity in heaven.

I was thirty-one and built like a truck by anyone's standards. But that night, I felt small—like a little boy. *His* boy.

And I wept with my entire body.

After the funeral, with only half a heart and a body that was racking up battle wounds, I returned to Tampa to re-enter football. Whatever tears I shed at the funeral were long dried by the time the plane touched down. I turned them off, shifting gears and putting on a mask to cover my pain.

Well, at least that's what I *tried* to do.

When my dad died, even though the tears dried, my emotional pain didn't. Instead, I tried to stuff it, but more often ended up medicating it away.

Without my dad to report to after my games, I felt no ambition to play. Football didn't feel like the same sport anymore.

Intellectually, I still had a purpose: *to stay in the game* to support my family and serve my beloved community. But emotionally, I was going through the motions, tossed around like a dirty sock in a washing machine. Except instead of getting clean, I became even more numb.

In November, Mom came to Florida for some family time at

a beautiful beach hotel. It was meant to rejuvenate and heal us. I tried to join my family and be present. But as I raised my arm to toss a ball to my kids, my body wouldn't cooperate. I screamed and fell flat on my back on the sand, seizing again. Lydia rushed around me, and the next thing I knew, I was carried away on a stretcher, with my kids and Mom standing wide-eyed as the surf beat behind them. Brady was only four at the time—too young to comprehend what was happening, but old enough to lock in a memory (to this day) of what it was like to see his daddy hauled away.

"Honey, there's something wrong with you," Lydia persisted in the ER as she nervously insisted to doctors and nurses that they get to the bottom of it. We awaited more tests, but nothing was found.

Desperate for answers, Lydia put the timeline together and realized that my seizures started after surgery. As I thought about it, I realized that the seizures happened when I went off Halcion. Right before Mom came to town, I had run out of meds, so I'd skipped a couple of doses, having another seizure.

I didn't know anything about withdrawals, and it still didn't occur to me that I had a problem. I just figured I better not go off those meds cold turkey again.

If I had stopped to think, I would have remembered that I was never good at moderation. Besides ending up on the evening news back in high school for my liquor store antics, in the pros, the night before the Bucs played the Saints in New Orleans, a few of us got into our bunks just in time for bed-check the night before a game. Then we snuck out, drinking all night. That little stunt got us in the record books for the longest drive ever. After winning the toss, we started a slow, steady, twenty-two-play offensive drive. Along the way, we accrued a bunch of penalties, which meant that we'd have to repeat the down. I didn't think we'd ever get off the field. Between plays, I puked like a sick dog, as did some of my teammates.

Had I ever taken a moment to reflect, I'd have realized that I didn't have an off switch. I did fine not drinking at all; but once I opened that door, I didn't stop. It didn't even matter if I had something as important as a game the next day.

Surely I don't have the same problem with the doctor-distributed drugs, I assured myself.

CHAPTER NINETEEN

THE INTERVENTION

*"Setting a goal is not the main thing. It is deciding how you
will go about achieving it and staying with that plan."*

—Tom Landry

December 19–20, 2018

Wilma said that Bobby usually stumbled in around two in the
morning and didn't get up until the early afternoon. So we
planned to arrive at Wilma's house by 6:50 a.m., hoping to wake
Bobby up at 7:00 a.m. for the intervention. With luck, Bobby,
Lydia, and I would be in Florida by dinnertime.

That night at the hotel, Lydia and I debriefed the family
session.

"Julia seems so broken," Lydia said as she rubbed lotion
into her hands. I could hear from her voice that Lydia was
reliving bad memories.

"I know this brings up some stuff for you," I told her. "And
I'm sorry for what I put you through. I'm glad we are here
together."

"I know that this isn't about me or us," Lydia interjected. "I'm grateful that we have a chance to help this family before they waste the next twenty years."

That stung. In her gentle way, Lydia was reminding me how I'd kept digging myself deeper into a hole. And I didn't stay alone in the pits; I brought the whole family down with me.

When I was a kid, the pastor preached a sermon on God's forgiveness that I still remember.

"There is nothing that you can do—no transgressions or sins, not even death, not angels or demons, nothing that is in this world or in the world to come—that can remove you from the love of God," he said. "So to the man who gets mad at his wife on a Saturday night, goes to the bar, drinks himself silly, gets into a brawl, and loses his eye in a fight, if that man were to wake up the next morning and ask God to forgive him, God will do it. God will wash that man's sins and make him whiter than snow. God would look upon that man as if he'd never sinned."

I remembered, too, the next thing the pastor said.

"God will forgive you, yes," the pastor repeated before adding the next part. "But He doesn't always choose to remove the consequences we reap. God will forgive the drunken brawler, but that man won't get his eye back."

One of my many consequences was that the pain I caused Lydia and my children didn't just disappear. Sometimes she still remembered that pain, and in those times, the hurt became fresh and raw again, almost like it just happened.

"I'm sorry," I told her, knowing there was nothing I could do to change the past. I was grateful I could be present with her on this night—and the many others I hoped to share with her.

Neither of us slept very well that night. I kept one eye on the clock, and I'm not sure what Lydia was thinking while she tried to sleep, but she tossed around enough for me to know that sleep wasn't coming easily to her either.

After showering and dressing for the day, we packed our

overnight bag. I sat in the stuffed chair next to the bed, and Lydia made us coffee from the little machine in the room. It made one cup at a time, and as she always does, she put herself second and brought me the first cup.

"Thanks, sweetie."

"You're welcome," Lydia returned pleasantly.

Even with two packets of sugar and powered creamer, the coffee tasted like dirt and rust.

"You feel ready for today?" I asked.

"Yeah," she said confidently. "I love seeing how God works."

Even when I'm in a bad mood or Lydia gets flooded with dark memories, I know what a lucky man I am to have her in my life. Besides my mom and God, no one would have put up with my crap as long as this woman has.

"I like the sound of that," I said cheerfully. "Let's see what God's got planned. Do you think there's any chance that us finding a Starbucks is part of His plan?"

She laughed as we headed out the door.

As luck had it, the town had two Starbucks. I let the GPS guide me to the closest one, and once we had some real coffee in hand, we headed to Wilma's. Moments after parking across the street as I'd done the previous night, Teddy and Allison pulled in the driveway. Then Robert pulled his truck behind ours.

Right on schedule, I thought. *We're almost ready.*

I waved and nodded from inside my vehicle as people arrived. By unspoken consensus, or more likely, insecurity about what we were about to do, we all sat in our cars waiting.

"This is when I start getting nervous," Lydia said, as I squeezed her hand.

Gary arrived, pulling behind Robert, and Julia found a spot on the driveway next to Teddy's car.

Taking that as our cue, I gave my wife's hand one more squeeze and opened my car door. The others followed suit. Our feet made muted sounds on the gravel soaked with recent rains. Over a couple of quiet "good mornings," we made our way to the door where Wilma had been waiting.

"He got home just before three o'clock," she whispered. "I heard him bumping into the kitchen table when he come in."

"Is it okay if we go to the seats we talked about last night?" I asked, using a similarly hushed voice. I did this more out of respect for the sober nature of our meeting and certainly not out of any belief that we'd wake Bobby.

"Sure," Wilma said quickly. Then she added, "I have a fresh pot of coffee if anyone needs any. Help yourself."

Once we gathered in our assigned seats, I looked around the room.

"Hey everybody," I began, scanning the room. "You've probably heard, 'It takes a village to raise a child.' It's clear you love Bobby, because you're here, despite his actions. Not everyone has such a strong village. If you feel uneasy, that's normal." Several heads nodded. "It reminds me of game day. We have a winning playbook and strong team. But Bobby may have a playbook of his own. So let's work together and stay calm when he pushes back. He'll keep us on our toes," I reinforced. "And one more thing. Would you mind if I asked God to guide us?"

I heard a chorus of affirmations like, "Sure. Absolutely. Please. That would be great. I agree."

No one, even atheists or agnostics, have ever refused my requests to seek God's help. When people have exhausted every option, they become more willing to ask for divine intervention.

"Dear Father," I prayed aloud, "Bobby is Your child. Please show him the love and grace that You've shown me and many others. And please help this family to heal. We ask that You guide our steps this morning. Use us to help Bobby."

"Amen," several people affirmed.

I leaned forward on my seat like a coach giving one last reminder of the plays to a team before entering the field.

"Okay, you all have your letters?" I asked.

Everyone except Robert nodded and said, "Yes," in a single voice.

Turning back to the rest of the family, I continued: "Do you have your list of things that you'll do differently if Bobby doesn't go into treatment?"

Gary shrugged. "Wrote down that the only honest reference I can give him today is that he worked for me. But I can't recommend him while he's still drinking."

"That works fine, Gary," I nodded. "Anyone else?"

Wilma raised her hand and then realized that she looked like a grade schooler and lowered it with a laugh. Everyone else chuckled nervously with her, releasing some tension.

"I thought about what you said." She returned to a serious tone. "You're right. He can't live here if he won't get help."

"Good for you," I told her sincerely. "I know that's not easy to say. And it's not easy to do, either. Let's hope it doesn't come to that."

"If he doesn't get help, I can't have him around Anna or in my life," Julia said without looking up. "I don't want to divorce him, but he's made me single with his drinking and whatever else he's doing…"

Julia's words cut off, and she bit her lip to keep it from trembling. Wilma, Allison, and Lydia instantly jumped up to comfort her. After a few minutes, everyone looked composed.

Lydia kept her arm around Julia's shoulder and said, "I know that's the last thing you want to do, honey. And I'm going to be praying the whole time that it doesn't come to that, that God will heal Bobby and restore your family."

The wall clock read 7:10. We'd showered, dressed, caffeinated, and already shed a few tears before the sun appeared in the sky. It dawned on me that if I were at home, I'd still be sound asleep.

"Okay," I said at last. "I'm ready. Are you all ready? Do you remember the order of who's going to read letters? Who's first?"

Allison raised her hand.

"Who's after Allison?"

"That would be me," Wilma said.

"And after Wilma?"

"I'm next," Robert said, shifting in his chair.

"And then it's me," Teddy offered without waiting to be asked.

"I'm after Teddy," Gary said.

"And then that leaves...?" I asked and waited.

Julia raised her hand without speaking.

"Okay, that's the order we'll follow," I told the group. "When Julia is done, I'll talk to him about getting into treatment today. He may argue and not want to go. That's okay. This is all new to him." I reassured everyone that I'd done this before and seen it all.

"If he outright refuses to go, I'll let him know that you all will set firm boundaries, so whether he gets help or not, things will change. And if it comes to that, we'll follow the same order we did reading the letters, okay?" I asked once I finished.

Heads nodded silently.

"So Wilma?" I pushed myself up from the chair using my arms. "Are you ready for us to get Bobby?"

"No," she said as she stood up. "Can we pray again?"

CHAPTER TWENTY

RANDY'S STORY

*"How lucky I am to have something that makes
saying goodbye so hard."*

—A.A. MILNE, WINNIE-THE-POOH

My luck began running on mere fumes, as I burned it up between handfuls of pills. But I remained determined to reignite any weak flame in my career, so I kept moving.

When you play in the NFL, your position is never a given. No matter how much camaraderie exists between teammates, one man's injury becomes another man's opportunity.

After my injury, I needed time to heal and rehab to regain my range of motion and strength. Then it was "go time"; I had to beat out the guy who'd filled in for me while I'd been out. He was younger, but fortunately, I had experience. So I got my spot back, and I entered my tenth year determined to kick ass.

A short time later, we faced Green Bay in the first home game of the season. The coach called for a pass play, which meant that after snapping the ball, I'd be giving the quarterback time to find an open man and complete the pass. After the snap, I faced the rusher across from me and locked him up. I didn't give him an inch. I was no rookie, and he was no Randy White. There would be no reaching around me to hit my quarterback as I crumbled like a ragdoll.

But then my leg slid. It felt weird because I didn't lose traction. My shoe hadn't moved; instead, my leg literally slipped out of my ankle. This was no sprain or twist. I'd had plenty of those. This was different. What I had was a severe dislocation.

My heart dropped into the ground as my body collapsed under its weight. I lay waiting for the doctors and trainers to get me off the field. I thought through the recovery in my head. I knew I wouldn't be out for just the rest of the game. It could be *weeks, months—or the rest of the season.*

Still, I was determined to give it an ol' Randy Grimes best effort. I showed up to practice just to treat my ankle and lift some weights. That's about all I could do. As far as game time, I couldn't participate. I sat in the press box, an outsider.

I kept lifting to stay strong. As much as my heart was no longer truly in the game, I didn't want to lose my position. Being a Tampa Bay Buccaneer was my touchstone, and I'd made it my identity. I wasn't ready to stop because I didn't know what else to do.

Part of what I loved so much about football was the locker room—which is a metaphor for the guys I got to know as my community. No matter how the game went, we were family. Those relationships held a lot together for me, even when things weren't going well in another area of life.

Without that camaraderie and support before, during, and after games, I got sucked towards a black hole. In my mental solitude, all I could think about was how much I missed my dad—and I grew more numb to everything around me. As more time passed, I no longer felt like I was part of the locker room. I felt more like an observer. And I began to feel very isolated.

"You'll get through this, Randy," Lydia reassured me with her concerned love. "You might even get sent to another team." But I knew better because I knew the stats. Most centers lasted two years. I was in my tenth season, with more than a hundred starts behind me. Getting picked up by another team would be like an old horse being rescued from the glue factory, and then winning the Triple Crown the next year. It would make a great story, but it would never happen.

My luck in other areas of my life began flickering into darkness. Earlier that same year in 1992, we'd bought a big house in Houston, then spent $30,000 on a pool big enough to host all our friends and family. Great house, huge debt, and terrible timing.

At the Christmas party in 1992, our offensive line coach said between bites with a laugh, "Well, Randy, you've milked this career another year. When are you going to stop *stealing from the team?*"

You SOB, I thought.

He was a great former Houston Oiler who everybody in Houston loved. Despite his reputation as a player, I wanted to choke him in that moment. But it wasn't because he was incorrect. It was because he *hit a nerve of truth.* He knew I'd been out half the year with my triceps surgery. Now I'd just been paid for another year with an ankle injury.

I'd never been that guy who wanted to be paid for contributing nothing. I'd given this team my blood, sweat, and tears—and the best years of my life. It paid me well, but in return, I'd sacrificed my body and taken on pain that would never go away.

His words reinforced more than ever that I was the outsider—even with my own team. I convinced myself they were just waiting for me to move on, that I no longer held value to them.

As much as his words hurt, they didn't shock me. I'd started to look at the organization in a more jaded way. We'd had an awful year on the field. Not surprisingly, we weren't headed for the championships. In fact, we didn't have a postseason in any of my years with the organization. We didn't draft well, we didn't sign free agents well, and there was no real commitment to win. During the eighties, the Bucs were one of the most profitable teams in the NFL, because the owner focused on saving money instead of going all the way to the Super Bowl.

As a result of that philosophy, the Bucs became a revolving door of coaches, players, front office people, and scouts. There was no real continuity, and that's what an organization requires to win. For example, in my ten years, I'd gone through five head coaches and six offensive line coaches. We had ten quarterbacks and four GMs. When new coaches came in, they'd build their team around players that they'd personally chosen in order to secure loyalty from those players. I was the best player for the position, so they played me. But it wasn't because they felt a sense of loyalty to me, Randy Grimes.

Since I'd spent my entire life playing and studying football, I had my own opinion about why the Bucs owners didn't try to make a bigger splash. It had to do with our media market. Years before Tom Brady came to Tampa, we weren't in New York, we weren't in L.A., and we weren't America's team: the Cowboys (and later I suppose you could add the Patriots). Heck, we weren't even the only team in Florida. We were the "other" Florida team, after the Dolphins.

But still, every game I played was an honor. Being an NFL player fueled my gratitude. And as bad as Tampa's record was while I played, I could never have asked for a better, more supportive community. Lydia and I absolutely fell in love with the town and its people, something neither of us expected when we left our native Texas.

We played our last game of the season that year in late

December. Since we were not heading to the playoffs, it was time to pack up our lockers and disappear for a few months until practice started the next year.

I turned in all my equipment and headed to my locker, the one right next to the exit door. All I had to do was clean it out and head home like all the other guys, and all the other years.

Time to head out, Randy, I told myself as I prepared to gather my things, reflecting briefly on the season. This was the ritual I'd done nine other times.

I could not have scripted or predicted what would happen next, even in my deepest moments of questioning my role on the team.

As I stood looking into my dark locker, I felt a big hand softly touch my shoulder. Somewhat startled, I froze.

Within that second, without turning around to see who it was, I heard a voice in my ear, "*Randy, we won't be needing your services next year.*" Those words were spoken with the same casual tone one might say, "Hey buddy, let's grab coffee next week."

I recognized Head Coach Wyche from his voice. He didn't wait for my response before hitting that metal bar that opened the exit door and walking out in one smooth movement. His words echoed in my ears, and I never saw his face or even the back of his head.

My heart dropped to my stomach. My palms sweated, and I grasped at the air, trying to feel something that resembled normalcy again.

Surely it can't end like that, I thought. I always knew my career wouldn't last forever. But when I pictured it ending, I thought it would be more on my terms. No, I didn't expect a Randy Grimes retirement parade, a street named after me, or a statewide Randy Grimes Day holiday. But after ten years, I also didn't expect my efforts to be dismissed with a movement as routine as turning out the light—by a guy who barely knew me.

I extended my arm into the dark locker and raked its contents into a black trash bag before exiting the back door. That was the last time I was ever in One Buc Place. After ten years of practically living there, it was over.

And I had no idea what was next.

CHAPTER TWENTY-ONE

THE INTERVENTION

"None of us, including me, ever do great things. But we can all do small things, with great love, and together we can do something wonderful."

—Mother Teresa

December 20, 2018

I followed Wilma to the room where Bobby slept. She paused in front of the door, then rapped three times before saying in the strongest voice she could muster, "Bobby? We need to talk with you."

We heard nothing from behind the door.

After knocking again, Wilma repeated herself more loudly, "Bobby, I need you to get up. We need to talk."

This time, we heard a moan.

"Bobby!" Wilma said harshly. "Either you answer me and get up, or I'm coming in!"

"I'm sleeping!" a voice grunted from inside.

Wilma looked at me for direction, and I mouthed the words, "Let's go in."

By the time Wilma swung open the door, Bobby had returned to a stupor of sleep. His room looked and smelled like a postgame locker room with clothes thrown across the floor and a sickly combination of liquor and sweat filling the air. Bobby sprawled out flat across the bed on his lean stomach, wearing nothing but boxers. His head turned to his left, facing the door.

Wilma sat on the bed next to him and rubbed his back like mothers do to small children.

"Bobby," she said in a quieter tone.

Bobby's body jerked, and he opened his eyes. Instead of his eyes resting on his mother, they landed on me standing between the bed and the door. I could see his mind begin to register that a very large stranger hovered over him, and he rolled to the side of the bed farthest from me and sprang up shouting.

"What the hell?!" he yelled, as he looked around for something to grab. I've done enough of these early morning drunken wake-up calls to have seen this reaction before. He was either looking for something to hit me with or his clothes. In this case, he found neither.

"Language, Bobby!" Wilma said sharply. "You didn't open the door, so we let ourselves in."

Bobby's eyes were still wide as he tried to figure out what was going on.

"This is Randy," Wilma said, remaining seated on Bobby's bed. "I've asked him to come here today so he could help us talk to you about your drinking."

I was impressed with how calm Wilma remained. Given that she had gone back and forth on Bobby even having a drinking problem, she showed strong resolve in her words and demeanor.

"Get out of here!" Bobby finally responded. "I don't know you!"

His tone took on an element of fear and desperation.

"Hi, Bobby," I said calmly. "No one is going to hurt you. We just want to talk with you a few minutes."

"Everyone is waiting in the family room," Wilma added.

Bobby picked a flannel shirt off the floor and punched his arms through the holes. He didn't bother to button it.

I've done interventions before where the person is so out of it, they storm out of their room in just underwear. One teenage girl came out wearing nothing but a thong. And it was on backwards. In times like that, I'm even more grateful that Lydia is with me. She is quick to find clothes to wrap around any half-naked, inebriated person.

"What the..." he started before correcting himself, "What are you talking about? Who's here?" Bobby asked incredulously. "Why are you doing this, Mom?"

"We will talk about this in the other room," Wilma said as she stood up. "Come join us, and I'll get you some coffee."

Dropping his arms to his side, Bobby sighed heavily and shook his head. "I don't want to talk to anyone."

Bobby blinked a few times and sat on the edge of his bed with his eyes still on me. After a moment, he picked up a pair of jeans from the floor and pulled them up to his knees. Finally, he stood and pulled his pants up.

"You better come in here, Bobby, or we're all going to come into your room to talk," Wilma shouted from another room.

Man, I thought. *Wilma couldn't be doing any better.*

After glaring at me for a few seconds while shaking his head, Bobby walked out of his room, giving me a wide berth and angry sideways glare.

As Bobby came into the family room, Allison patted the seat on the sofa next to her.

"Come sit next to me, Bobby," she offered.

Bobby blinked a few times while his eyes focused on those who had gathered in the family room. His face took on the appearance of a trapped animal. He rubbed his cheeks roughly with his hands. When he finished, he looked around and realized that he was not only awake, but also having a nightmare.

Now that he stood in the light, I got a better look at him. My first thought of Bobby's appearance was that if he gained thirty pounds, he could be a Calvin Klein model. Like his mom and sister, he had dark hair that he wore close-cropped, like a baseball player. His face showed a week's worth of stubble. His eyes, while streaked with red veins, looked to be a blue-gray. I guessed him to be maybe two inches shorter than me, putting him at around 6'2". But Bobby's frame had slid past lean into skinny. It didn't help that his jeans fell below his waist, having no butt to hold them up.

"Okay, I don't know what the hell you all are doing here, but you can get out, d'you hear me?" Some of his words slurred together.

"We just want to talk with you for a few minutes," I told him, positioning myself between the family room and the kitchen, his nearest escape route.

"Seriously, who the..." he started. "I don't know you, okay? What is this? An *intervention*?" he spat out sarcastically.

"Yes, Bobby," I responded truthfully. "That's exactly what this is. Your mom called me, and all these people wanted to let you know how much they care about you."

Wilma returned from the kitchen with a mug full of coffee.

"Here you go, honey," she said, holding it out to her son.

Instead of taking the offered cup, Bobby's folded his arms, his lean frame mostly covered by the flannel shirt.

Wilma didn't react, and set the mug on the coffee table next to Julia and within reach of where Allison wanted Bobby to sit.

"I put your coffee next to your wife when you're ready for it," she said, finding her own seat.

Bobby scowled at his mother. I figured that he didn't have any special anger at her, but she may have been the most convenient person to react to since she'd been the last person to talk. Finally, Bobby turned around and headed back to his room.

"This is bullshit!" he yelled without turning back.

Bobby's family looked at me as if to ask, "What now?"

"It's fine," I told them. "He might need to cool off for a minute."

On a hunch, I turned to Wilma and Julia.

"Does Bobby smoke?"

"He used to," Julia answered.

"Well," Wilma contradicted, "He's been smoking here."

Julia shook her head and flared her nostrils as she inhaled sharply.

"Not much, really," Wilma quickly added. "I seen him smoking on the porch a few times, and some nights he comes home smelling like cigarettes."

"I'll go check on him," I said, turning around and walking back to Bobby's room.

From the doorway, I saw him digging around the floor into a coat pocket.

"Hey," I said, making Bobby jump a bit. "I was going to step out back and have a chew. Do you want to join me before we get started?"

"I need a smoke," he said, throwing down the coat he'd been rifling through and picking up a leather jacket as he padded down the pockets.

Finally, he pulled out a crumpled, soft pack of Newports and a white lighter.

"Come on," I said casually. "Put that coat on. It's cold out there."

Bobby sighed but slipped into his coat.

"I don't need a babysitter," he said, pushing past me.

Despite the insult, I followed Bobby to the porch where he lit up and faced the back fence. The sky turned from a dark to light grey as dawn approached, and the pre-light temperatures felt frigid to me.

I pulled out my can of chew and placed a pinch between my lower lip and gums.

Filthy habit, I reminded myself. *But it gives me an excuse to sit alone with Bobby.*

We didn't talk. Some clients wake up so out of it that they talk a mile a minute, or they try to grab some car keys to make a run for it. Once a guy punched me, but immediately wished he hadn't. Movies make punches look easy, but that's because they're fake. When that guy hit me in the chest with his fist, his wrist snapped back, and he yelled in pain as if I'd been the one throwing the punch. We finished the intervention with him holding a bag of ice to his wrist. And one time, a guy pulled out a gun. But that's a story for another day.

As I glanced at this frail man sucking his cigarette like it contained nutrients he needed, I related to him. He just didn't know it yet.

CHAPTER TWENTY-TWO

RANDY'S STORY

"How can I let go of my dream when
it's the only dream I have?"

—RANDY GRIMES

Just like Bobby's pain likely got worse with the loss of his dad, so did mine.

When I lost my dad, I lost half of my heart. When I lost football two years later, I lost myself. I didn't know what to do with my time or life. I didn't have anybody helping me transition after football—into a different life. Dad would have been great for that. Without him, I felt I had no room to grieve, no one to guide me into the next phase.

Fortunately, we still had a little money in the bank. Since I'd only had one job since leaving college, I always had a steady and growing income. But I was in my early thirties. If I lived anywhere near the normal life expectancy of seventy-five years for a man, I had a long time left, and I knew that money wouldn't last. And sadly, when I made good money, I didn't count every penny. I didn't have a good handle on how expensive it would be to live without cash pouring in.

At least we would no longer need to cart the whole family back and forth between Tampa and Houston. Since we'd just moved in and completed our perfect home, we moved back to Houston, planning to settle in for the duration.

While I didn't have a firm plan of what to do after leaving football, for years I'd talked with my agent about joining him after I left the game. Even though we never really ironed out the details, I knew that he lived in a nice place in Chicago and was still connected to sports. Becoming an agent became my new dream.

Maybe this will all work out, I told myself.

We all have "good times" friends, people who come around when you're living large and doing well. But once you step off the pedestal, those friends disappear like a water mirage coming off a hot Texas highway. When my football career ended, I quit hearing from my agent. That hurt. I thought we were pretty close. He'd spent so much time with us, and he was someone I could call at any time. I'd been building a back-up plan based on working with him. Now I'd have no one showing me the ropes.

So I just did my best on my own. I visited several colleges and met with athletes, starting at my alma mater, Baylor. But I never got traction. Without a mentor, all I knew how to do was shake a lot of hands and meet talented players.

While I played football, Lydia had stayed at home with the kids, savoring the experience of being a full-time mom. She trusted I would figure things out.

But I didn't. Four years after leaving football, we were almost broke. Having always been the provider for the family, it took me a long time to turn to Lydia for help.

One day, Lydia had an idea for me. "Randy, my brother

works for a concrete business in town. They are always looking for good people," she said. "Why don't you go talk to them?"

After a short conversation with the owner, he said, "I can pay you thirty-eight grand a year."

"Okay, well thank you for your time. I'm sorry, but I can't do that," I said as I shook his hand politely.

Forget concrete, forget that owner, and forget that outrageous offer, I thought as I got back in my truck. *I can make ten times that much, and I'm worth twenty times more,* I told myself.

"Well?" Lydia asked, all smiles as I came through the door later that day. "Tell me how it went!"

"How did it go? That bozo offered me thirty-eight grand a year, that's how it went," I said in a huff. "Shoot, I'd rather volunteer."

"Well, babe," Lydia responded, "I'm going to pray tonight that God will show you where He wants you to work. But it might just be that He's opened a door for you."

"Are you saying you think I should take it?" I was almost afraid of the answer.

I didn't want to think I was that desperate, but I was. True to her word, Lydia prayed that God would show me the way. The next day, I went back to the cement company. I begged the owner for the job I'd politely declined not twenty-four hours earlier.

I'm not in the NFL anymore, I acknowledged to myself.

That was 1996. For the next three years, I would sell concrete. To say that my heart wasn't in it would be a profound understatement. Bitterness corroded me. I'd sit on a job and tell myself, "You've got to be kidding me. This is what the rest of my life looks like? Instead of bright lights and adoring fans, I'm getting white lung and being bossed around by idiots who barely have a GED."

Despite my job, money was still tight. "Babe," I started with my eyes down—and if had a tail, it would have been between my legs—"I hate to say this, but I think you're going to have to go back to work until I figure out a job." Lydia began teaching in 1997 without complaint.

It was my own ego, not cement dust, which blinded me from any gratitude that could have pulled me out of my funk.

I had one comfort during this dark time: my pills. Even though I couldn't justify them as a way to keep playing football, a seed of addiction had taken deep roots. But I didn't know it. When the pills weren't enough to keep my soul numb, I'd occasionally add other drugs. Once I took a combination of pills that left me sleeping while standing up.

I took opiates whenever I could get them, but benzos were still my staple. It had been Halcion, but I moved on to Ativan, and eventually Xanax. The pharmacies never stopped supplying me.

That habit I'd been able to keep under control for years slowly started showing itself to those around me. Lydia began saying things like, "Randy, I can't understand you. Why are you slurring?" Other times she'd ask, "What's wrong? Why are you so worked up?"

What I should have taken as a gentle prompt from a wife who loved me, I took as criticism. But guilt started eroding my self-worth. Fortunately, I had the solution: I started mixing in other drugs to block out my shame.

Before Christmas, I snorted cocaine and stayed up all night decorating. While Lydia was used to seeing me sleepy, she wasn't used to seeing me cranked up on coke. She didn't know who I was, not that I knew at the time either. I still went to work, but my life quickly became a full-time side game of getting more drugs to get through the day.

The cliches might tell you that the worst drugs are found only in the outskirts and back alleys of the most dangerous cities, but that's not the case. I found a cocaine dealer around the corner in my respectable neighborhood. He was a "nice guy," letting me buy stuff on credit and pay him later. He rode a loud motorcycle that I could hear from blocks away. He never came looking for me to "pay up now or else," but I think he'd roar by my home from time to time to remind me that he knew where I lived.

As a kid, I'd played by the rules. As a teen growing up in Tyler, I'd hung out with fellow athletes and didn't cause trouble. At Baylor, I'd got crazy drunk a few times with some teammates, but for the most part, I'd stuck with good, solid people who shared my values. Even in the NFL, I'd colored within the lines, so to speak. I took pills my doctors and trainers gave me. I'd always been considered an upstanding man and pillar of the community.

Not anymore. I'd become Randy Grimes, the guy who shows up at a local cocaine dealer's house, takes down a brick of coke, busts off a piece, weighs it, puts it in a baggie, and walks back home as casually as someone who'd just bought a bag of oranges at Albertsons.

At least I'm not buying drugs from some creep on the shady side of town, I told myself.

I continued down this very dark hole that had become my life, at the same time Lydia did everything in her power to give our kids the best life she could. She cleaned the house from top to bottom for all the parents who were coming over for pictures. Then she helped my sweet and beautiful daughter, Emily, get all dolled up for a Christmas dance.

For my part, I had no idea what Emily wore to her big dance. I couldn't tell you what her date looked like, even if you'd asked me the next day. I had no way of noticing if the house had been cleaned or not. That's because I disappeared sometime during the day, snorting cocaine and drowning myself in rum. I hung out with my next-door neighbor, knowing I couldn't show my face at home. By the time he brought me home, I was hammered. The neighbor told Lydia I was on cocaine, and she reports being shocked, although my memories of the episode were like underexposed snapshots—dim and impossible to make out.

It wasn't the first time I'd snorted cocaine, so I had stories. When my nose would run, I'd tell Lydia it was because of the "stray cats" that would get into our garage. "Dang allergies," I'd say.

When the neighbor outed me, my charade was over, but I was too messed up to care.

The drugs were warring in my brain, and I lost it. I could pass a lie detector that I don't remember my next moves, but according to Lydia, I attacked the oven, trying to rip off the oven door. Ripping out the burners, I tossed them around the kitchen, flinging them through the air like they were decorative pillows. Then I threw the kitchen chairs across the house as if I were defending myself against ghosts. In the process, I smashed up Lydia's beloved Santa salt and pepper shaker against the kitchen floor.

"Satan, get off my back!" I growled with each movement. "Get off my back!" I felt like someone was strangling me.

Lydia prayed and pleaded with me to calm down. Then she called her dad and brother to come over. Together, they got me into bed.

Once I was passed out in bed, Lydia asked her brother to pick up the kids at the dance and take them out to eat—giving her time to clean up and me time to be completely out. Even with the stress I heaped on her, her first instinct was to protect the kids from seeing their father like this. She didn't want them around me in that state. But she still stayed with me, scared of what might happen next.

I woke up in bed with no memory of the night before.

That year, we went to Austin for Christmas. On Christmas morning of 1999, I got bit by a spider on my shin. My lower leg got huge, and the sore festered and oozed. That's when Lydia found a straw in the bathroom. A light clicked on inside her head. She realized it was for coke.

On the way home, the spider bite kept getting worse. While Lydia drove us home, I spread out in the backseat. I smeared cocaine on the spider bite, thinking somehow that would help.

I ended up in the ER, where the doctor identified my bite as from a brown recluse spider. As its poison spread, it broke down my tissue, forming an ulcer around the bite. I spent six days in the hospital as the doctors cut away the rotted tissue. I nearly lost my leg.

While I battled to keep my leg, Lydia fought to save my life. She'd seen the monster unleashed inside me. She'd witnessed my rampage while on cocaine.

Pulling my doctor aside, she told him everything she knew.

"We could just ship him from here to there," the doctor said, referring to a treatment center. "But," they said, "Randy must be *willing* to go."

My family decided to confront me in my hospital bed.

"Randy, Honey. We love you, and we're worried about you," Lydia said as Mom stood near her.

"It's going to be fine," I reassured her. "The doc cut out enough infected tissue that he can save the leg. I should be out of here in a couple more days."

"This is not about the bite," she continued. "I know what you've been doing. The cocaine. I don't know when this started, but I think you need to get some help to beat these drugs."

"Listen," I nodded. "I will admit that I've let things get out of hand. And I'm sorry for all of that," I said. "I'll straighten it out. I promise. You'll see." I reached to squeeze Lydia to reassure her that everything would be okay, but she didn't immediately respond. *Maybe she is starting to get sick of this,* I thought.

It wasn't an intervention, but it was as close to one as anyone had ever done for me. But without any big conse-quences to me, I had no motivation to follow through.

I recovered from the spider bite, and things went back to normal. By normal, I don't mean that I stopped using cocaine— or benzos, or opiates, or alcohol. I mean I slipped into my new norm, where I would lay low for a week or two, going through the motions so that my family would get off my back. Then I would binge again, escaping into hell for a few days.

It's not that I was trying to manipulate my family, but I knew the drill: I'd tell myself I had it under control. I'd convince myself and everyone that I was better. Then I'd relax whatever part of my brain was white knuckling it to stay sober. Willpower is a muscle that weakens with overuse. Once exhausted, I'd chase my next high as if my life depended on it.

I was far away from handing over my will to my higher power, Jesus Christ. Instead, I'd defend what was coming into focus as my *addiction*.

CHAPTER TWENTY-THREE

THE INTERVENTION

December 20, 2018

Watching Bobby smoking on the back porch, I didn't get a sense that I intimidated him in the least. Bobby seemed like a guy who kind of knew that something was coming, and he'd almost resigned himself to his fate. I just stayed quiet. Opening my mouth might push him from quiet compliance to active rebellion.

Bobby took long draws on his cigarette and blew out clouds of smoke that the wind brought over his shoulder directly in my face. Even from a few feet away, the combination of the cold air and smoke burned my eyes. I spit over the rickety railing and waved the smoke away.

When he finished his smoke, he dropped the butt onto the porch, ground it out with the heel of his bare foot, and kicked it to the ground below. Looking around, I saw several other cigarette butts littering the property—at his mother's home.

My eyes never got used to the sting from smoke. Even if I'd wanted to become a smoker—and as an athlete, I never wanted anything to take away my wind—burning eyes would keep me from blowing an acrid flame out of my mouth.

Looking back at Bobby, I saw that he had lit another cigarette. Instead of sucking this one down, he seemed to be using it as a prop, something to stall his return to the house.

Delay of game, I chuckled.

As I looked at Bobby in the gathering light, his skin looked grey and very different from the pictures I'd seen in Wilma's house. In those photos, Bobby's skin wore a bronze tone, and his easy smile reached into his bright eyes. He looked nothing like that at this moment.

There but by the grace of God, go I, I thought before correcting myself by adding, *and went I*. It hadn't been that long since I could have been right there with Bobby.

My heart went out to Bobby. I knew what it was like to disappoint family and friends to the point of feeling like there was nowhere to go.

Bobby watched me out of the corner of his bloodshot eyes. "Let's get this over with so I can go back to sleep," he said as he rubbed out the last of his smoldering cigarette.

"Sounds good," I said with a wide smile as I took a final spit off the porch, holding the door open.

Seconds later, Bobby turned his back and walked inside to his waiting family, as dawn broke on the cold morning.

CHAPTER TWENTY-FOUR

RANDY'S STORY

"The marks humans leave are too often scars."

—JOHN GREEN

"Mom, I don't know what to do!" Fifteen-year-old Emily shouted into the phone when she called Lydia out of class. "Dad's on the kitchen floor, and he won't get up!" Lydia had a hard time understanding Emily through her gasps and screams. Emily was old enough to know this was not a normal situation, but young enough to be completely traumatized by what she saw.

"Emily, try to stay calm. Is he okay?" Lydia tried to reason with Emily, as the kids shouted in the classroom behind her.

"No, he's *not* okay!" Emily shouted. "Nana's here, too. Daddy's pants are down, and he must have fallen over. Now we can't get him up," she said.

"Randy, just get up!" Lydia's mother screamed.

Lydia raced home. By the time she got there, I was sitting up, answering to a growing group of family members who kept filing in.

"Yeah, okay," I admitted to Lydia's brother. "I did take some drugs."

Like there could be any other explanation other than insanity. I'd say whatever I could to get out of this situation, even if it meant telling an occasional truth.

Lydia packed a bag for me and grabbed her purse. *This can't be good,* I thought. I had no leverage. I'd seen some strange things in my day, but I'd never seen something like what I'd just done. I had no choice but to follow her to the car.

She took me downtown to St. Joseph's, where I was kept overnight locked in a room with a bubble window in the door. Lydia feared for my life, and at that time, the only way she could feel safe was putting me in someone else's care.

I lay in bed that night, wide-eyed with fear that *I'd have a seizure if I didn't get some Halcion soon.*

Back at home, my family spent the night clearing the house of guns, fearing that my next rampage could turn in a direction that couldn't be reversed.

The next morning, I suppressed the demons growing inside of me long enough to turn on my charm offensive. I sweet-talked the staff and got released. As a center protecting my quarterback, I learned to be efficient in my brutality. But as a drug addict in hiding, I traded in brute force for sweetness and charm to get what I wanted. Lydia reluctantly took me home, very disappointed that I wouldn't get help.

A few months later, Lydia and I planned a very special party for Emily's sweet sixteen. Unfortunately, I remember only two things surrounding that day.

Number one: I bought Emily a brand-new red Mustang. My credit was just good enough to do that. But it got stolen out of our driveway the second night she had it.

"Was it one of your cocaine buddies?" she asked. My heart dropped into my stomach.

"No," I answered. She didn't look convinced.

We found it a week later at the Astrodome, and it was perfectly fine. Someone had taken a joyride in it, and we got it back.

But that wasn't the worst thing that happened on her birthday.

That leads me to *number two:* With no recall of the day, I woke up on the evening of her birthday in my La-Z-Boy with wet jeans from the knees down.

Lydia remembers a lot more about that night. I was supposed to show up with a karaoke machine for Emily's slumber party. As Lydia was bustling about getting ready, there was a knock on the door. There I was, high as a kite—and drenched. Lydia saw a truck drive away, hauling a boat.

"What in the heck happened to you?" she asked, pulling me inside. I couldn't tell her. She plopped me into my chair, as the girls started showing up.

"What's wrong with Dad?" Emily asked. Lydia distracted her long enough to move me to the bedroom, where I slept all night. She'd gotten good at hiding the damage and pretending like nothing had happened—just like my mom's mom and dad's mom had done decades before. The party went on without me.

By the grace of God, Lydia's brother, Johnny, spotted my truck in a lake ten miles away. We called a wrecker to haul it home. Her brother did not typically drive down that road, but he had done so seemingly randomly that day.

I would never remember driving on the road, let alone driving into a lake. And whoever dropped me off at home must have been someone we knew, because whoever it was knew where I lived.

That was my work truck, and it was all mucked up with mud and water. The guys from the concrete plant came to my house and got it running again. Corporate never heard a whisper of it, I don't think.

Eventually, though, there was a separate investigation at work into the rampant drug use, and I got canned. They asked me not to come in for my last two weeks.

Two months later, I landed another job—this time at a brick company. At work, I focused on the job, grew my accounts, showed up on time, and did everything asked of me.

I tried to make it work. I went to bed early enough to wake up clear-headed. When Lydia started leading children's church, I started helping, teaching the youth while Lydia shepherded them.

I told myself *this is progress*. But in reality, I never stopped using.

In case anyone cared to look, I wore a good face. It's like how we use a social media profile photo showing an idealized, digitally enhanced, perfect self—instead of the accurate one that reveals us looking bloated, pale, and stupid.

But try as I might to act the part of *normal*, there were cracks in my façade.

I was coaching Brady in Little League, as I'd done since he was four. But I was so messed up, I would slur at games. Parents were starting to notice.

As I got ready to drive home after a particular practice, Brady, Emily, her future husband, and Lydia's nephew jumped into the truck, and the kids got into the bed. On the way home, I blacked out. The truck, however, continued flying down a really long street, and I ran a red light. The kids hung on for dear life. When I came to, I pulled into a gas station.

A close call.

We began to face financial ruin.

"Lydia," I said after I could no longer avoid the inevitable, "We can't afford this house. The numbers don't add up. We have to find something smaller." And by smaller, I meant cheaper.

If you were to ask me nine years prior if I'd ever sell that house, I'd have told you in a menacing voice, *"Over my dead body."*

You see, that house wasn't just a home to Lydia and the kids for nine years. It was a symbol of my success. It was our dream. It was where our entire family congregated, joyfully. When I signed and handed over the papers, I signed away much more than just a piece of real estate.

When I lost my dad, I lost my direction. When I lost football, I lost my purpose. And when I lost my home, I lost my *man card*, my self-worth.

God had gifted me with a loving family, despite my failures. But I could not see that I offered value to anyone else. I stayed blinded by foolish pride and drugs.

The day before we moved out of our beloved house, I took some pills. I think it was morphine, but to be honest, the specific drug no longer mattered. I'd gotten into the habit of hoarding a hodge-podge of pills into the same bottle, knowing that whatever I took would in some way help numb my pain.

But that wasn't the first handful of pills I'd taken that day. Between the grief and chaos of moving, I'd double-dosed. At the time, I considered this an accident. But a friend recently asked if maybe I did it to escape all that was crashing down on me, and I can't confidently refute that possibility.

As I slipped into bed that night next to Lydia, I fell into a dream where I was trying to talk to Dad over the phone. I'd just finished a big game, and I'd not played well. We didn't have good reception, and the line popped with buzzes and pops. I kept talking louder and more slowly to penetrate the static. Finally, I heard a few words break through.

"Can't...hear...come over...we'll talk."

CHAPTER TWENTY-FIVE

THE INTERVENTION

"Holding onto something that is good for you now, may be the very reason why you don't have something better."

—C. JoyBell C.

December 20, 2018

Bobby's life was about to come to a crossroads. Like me, he'd been wearing his relationships thin.

"Before you all tell me what a failure I am," Bobby started talking while standing in the doorway facing his family and Gary, "Let me just say that I know I've had some problems. I lost my job," he looked directly at Gary, "And the other jobs were just a waste of time."

"Bobby, sit the hell down!" his grandfather, Robert, said in a raised voice. "We just wanna talk to you is all," he added, softening his tone.

"Fine," Bobby said defiantly as he dropped hard on the couch.

"Lecture me, tell me what a terrible son and grandson I am. Tell me what a loser of a father and husband I am," he directed at his wife Julia. "Tell me I'm an asshole," he said, looking towards Teddy. "Tell me I'm not worth shit!"

"Bobby," I said, keeping my voice soft.

"And who the hell is *that*?" he said when he saw Lydia in the room. "The Avon Lady?"

Lydia let a disarming, small smile cross her face.

"No, I'm Randy's wife," Lydia said sweetly. "I'm here for moral support for y'all."

"So Bobby," I continued, "Your mom would like to share what we're all doing here."

Bobby slouched back in the sofa and rolled his head towards his mother. His eyes didn't reach hers; instead, he stared at the ceiling.

"I love you, Bobby," Wilma began. "We all do. That's why we're here. But I'm worried about you."

"Mom, you don't have to worry about me," Bobby interrupted. "I'm fine. I don't have a problem with drinking or drugs. So this is a waste of everyone's time."

Wilma continued as if Bobby hadn't spoken.

"I didn't know what to do. I was talking with Laverne who used to go to our church before she moved to Houston. Do you remember her?" she didn't pause for Bobby to answer. "Anyway, she told me that Randy and Lydia came to her house about two years ago. They talked with Laverne's daughter, Alana, who was doing heroin."

Bobby didn't speak. His jaw remained firm, and his red eyes glared into space.

"Heroin," Wilma repeated. "Alana had been arrested several times and tried to quit on her own. But she kept going back to those drugs," Wilma shook her head as she spoke. "And I got to thinking about you and your accident," she continued.

"I take pills for pain, Mom," Bobby cut in. "I'm not a drug

addict. You have no idea what you're talking about. I have *pain!*"
he yelled again.

Within minutes, Bobby went from having no drinking or
drug problem to admitting that he did take pills, but just for
pain.

"So I called Randy," Wilma finished. "Randy and Lydia got
Alana into treatment, and now she's doing great. Alana's even in
school studying to be a counselor."

"Good for her," Bobby said in a smarmy tone as he leaned
forward. "Can I go now?"

"Bobby," I jumped in. "You don't know me from Adam. As
your mom said, I help people get help for alcohol or drug
dependency. This morning is not about me; it's about you.
But let me tell you another reason your mom called me. I
spent many years strung out on drugs, pushing away my
wife, losing everything, including the respect of my
children."

"Oh, God," Bobby sighed, rolling his eyes as he pounded his
head against the couch.

"That doesn't qualify me for squat. What does, though, is
that I'm sober today. If I can do it, anyone can. And before you
argue, I never said that you have a drug or alcohol problem.
How would I know that? So instead of me talking with you, I
asked these folks who love you to share their thoughts...I know
you want to go back to bed, and I don't blame you," I said
sincerely. "I've been there. But first, you owe it these people to
hear them out."

"Blah blah blah," Bobby said under his breath.

"Allison?" I prompted. "Would you start?"

Reaching into her purse, Allison took out her cell phone
and put it on her lap.

"I typed it into my phone," she explained. "Our printer
broke, and my handwriting is awful. So Bobby," Allison started.
"Bobby?"

Instead of facing her, Bobby said between his teeth, "I can hear you with my ears."

"I'm just going to read it to you, okay?" Allison asked as she pulled up her letter. "Here goes."

After taking a deep breath, she began.

Dear Bobby,

I was only three when you were born, so I don't remember saying this. But Momma told me that when she brought you home from the hospital, I said, "Isn't our baby beautiful, Momma?" And growing up, all my friends were in love with you and wanted to date you.

And it wasn't just because you were handsome. You played baseball, made good grades without trying, were nice to everyone, made people laugh, and even the teachers liked you. I, on the other hand, was a giant pimple in high school, never played sports, worked hard for Bs, and I'm not sure my teachers would even remember me.

You always knew how to put people at ease. In that way, I always looked up to you even though you were my little brother. You had something I didn't have, and I envied you.

We were close, but we got even closer after Daddy died. Momma told us that parents should always die before their children, because that was the proper order. Then she told us something I'll never forget. She said that she had two children so that we would never be alone, because we'd always have each other.

I guess that's why we got closer. We needed each other more. I remember when you stood up in my wedding, how handsome you looked. And I remember when you fell in love with Julia. I loved her immediately, and now she's like the sister I never had. Watching you fall in love made me so happy. You and I would sit up and talk for hours, even though we lived fifteen minutes apart. And then you told me you were expecting a baby! I couldn't have been happier than if it were happening to me.

For about ten years, we were inseparable, but then you faded away. I miss you, Bobby.

At first, I thought maybe you just had a string of bad luck when you got hurt, then lost your job. I know you've gotten tickets for drunk driving, and I thought you were depressed. But now you're living here instead of with Julia and Anna. It's like the things that should be most important to you just aren't anymore.

Then you got in that accident with Teddy's truck. For the first time, I started worrying about you, thinking, "Oh my God. What if something happens to Bobby, and he gets killed? What would I do? Could I ever forgive myself for not saying something?"

Anyway, I love you and still look up to you, Bobby. But I want my brother back.

I know you are hurting, probably in ways I don't even understand. But I know that you don't have to live like this. And no one wants to see you die like this.

Please, Bobby. I know how strong you are. But right now, I don't think being strong is enough. You need help. Please go to treatment.

I watched every face in the room while Allison read. Several people nodded their heads at different times. Wilma and Julia teared up a couple of times. Even Lydia worked to hold back tears, as some of what Allison said sounded too familiar.

Bobby's features were hard when Allison started reading. As she continued, he shrugged at a couple of points. By the time she finished reading, his mouth froze in a frown, but his eyes looked softer. I knew that face. Bobby wasn't mad. He was hungover, maybe even still intoxicated. He probably fought to stay awake. More than that, though, I could see the love from Allison's letter cover Bobby's anger like paint. I hoped enough of his sister's words broke through to make Bobby long to return to better times.

From Bobby's response, I felt confident that he would hear everyone out.

Wilma read an equally powerful letter, but she added a few things.

"I know what it's like growing up with a father who drank," Wilma said. "I don't remember seeing your grandpa drink, but my sister does. Sometimes when I was real little, I'd hear yelling and get scared. She'd climb into bed with me and hold me, saying everything would be okay." Wilma teared up.

At this point, Robert sniffed and wiped a tear from his own eye, too.

"I know how crushed you were when your father left and died," she continued as tears rolled freely.

Bobby worked hard to contain his tears at the mention of his dad.

"I know you don't want to put Julia and Anna through that same pain you felt," she read. "Julia is a godsend, like a second daughter to me. Only now I don't hardly see her 'cause of what you're doing. Your daddy died. He didn't mean to leave you. But now you're doing the same thing to Julia, and it ain't fair to her." Her voice cracked.

Bobby bit his lip as the words registered. Big, wet tears rolled down his face as his mother finished.

With his granddaddy, Robert, up next, I started getting a little worried that Robert might undo Bobby's state of mind.

Robert leaned forward in his chair and looked Bobby directly in the eyes.

"Look at me, boy," he said.

Bobby turned to face his grandfather.

"When I hear 'bout you stealing, hitting your momma, wrecking cars, and leaving Julia and Anna to fend for themselves, I wanna slap the whiskers off your face," he started.

So much for starting with the positives, I thought.

I relaxed, though, when he continued.

"It's hard to watch. From what I hear, you're doing the same stupid things I did when I'd hide inside a bottle instead of facing life like a man," he said.

Robert sat back in his chair, and his face relaxed.

"Julia needs you just like I needed my daddy. But my daddy died when I was just a little older than Anna, 'cause he did the same crap you're doin'. He wrecked his car driving drunk. You see why I get so mad when I hear what you're doin'?"

Bobby and Allison both seemed surprised to hear that. While alcoholism is often a family disease, passed through generations, many families are too ashamed to share all the sordid details.

"If I hadn't quit drinking," Robert said to Bobby, "Who knows if I wouldn't have died the same way."

After a slight pause, Robert continued.

"Your momma's right. I tried to drink away all the crap," he said. "The more I drank, the worse I felt. You said that you thought we were going to say you're a rotten dad? Well, get in line, son. I don't remember *seeing* my kids most mornings, I was so drunk from the night before. And then I'd come home hammered after they's already in bed."

Robert paused again and sipped his coffee.

"I stole from my boss," he said, keeping his eyes in front of him. "I never got caught, but I done it. Should have been fired. Hell, should have been sent to jail. I even..." he started, then swallowed a few times before continuing. "I even cheated on your grandmother."

At this statement, eyebrows shot up across the room.

"Oh, but I was drunk at the time, so it don't count, right?" Robert repeated aloud the lie he told himself those many years ago.

"But do you know I carry the guilt from what I done every day?" Robert said. "And I ain't had a drink for almost fifty years."

When I heard Robert say that, the words of the late, great comedian George Carlin came to mind: *Just because you got the monkey off your back doesn't mean the circus has left town.* Robert may have conquered his need to drink, but the guilt, shame, and anger in his eyes at times meant that part of him remained at the addiction circus. Some in recovery would call Robert a *dry drunk.* That's someone who still shows the actions and attitudes of addiction, just without the drugs or alcohol.

I wanted Bobby to do more than face his pain and addiction; I wanted to help him deal with his damaged emotional and spiritual demons, to live his best life.

"Don't be an idiot like me, boy," Robert said, his voice sounding gentler than I'd heard it before. "Don't lose every-thing—like this beautiful girl here." He pointed to Julia. "And that little daughter of yours, you hear? Quit while you still got things to live for."

Somber faces filled the room as Robert finished.

Teddy read next, telling Bobby how much he missed fishing with him. But he ended by laying things directly on the line:

The Bobby I know borrowed lots of things from me. You borrowed my chainsaw once and drove the bar into the ground so far you destroyed the chain and bar. Before you brought it back, you replaced it, so it was better than when I gave it to you. Every time you've used my boat, you've left it gassed up for me. And the few times you used my truck to haul stuff, you filled it and washed it before bringing it back. That's the Bobby I know.

But now, you don't seem to care about no one but yourself. You steal from your momma, spend money you don't have, walk out on your wife and little girl, and do nothing but drink. And then you slam my truck in the ditch drunk, but you don't even have the guts to tell me. You have your momma tell Allison, which is not the kind a thing a man does.

I'm still mad as hell about my truck. But you know what I'm even more mad about? You don't care that Allison and your mom are worried sick about you. You married a great a woman and have such a sweet little girl. But the only thing that matters to you is you. You are drinking yourself to death, and all we can do is watch. You need help, Bobby, and I hope to God you get it today.

I watched Bobby's face while Teddy spoke, and I saw it morph from anger to fear to sorrow. He was listening, that I could tell.

Gary's letter was short on words, but long on impact. He wrote it to his former employee and current friend in such a way that it sounded like a conversation instead of simple words on a page.

"When your daddy died, I felt like part of me did, too. At first, I spent time with you out of respect for your dad. But in no time, you became the son I never had. We had some good times, didn't we? Remember when you thought a bear was gonna kill us when we were camping at Payton Lake? We thought we were goners. But it wasn't a bear, was it? What was it, Bobby?" Gary asked.

"A deer," Bobby answered with a small smile as he remembered it.

"A deer licking the salt off our tent," Gary repeated. "When it's dark, every sound seems more terrifying. And you know what I think? I think it feels like it's dark outside. I know you're scared, and you don't think you'll make it. Maybe a part of you doesn't care if you do. But I know you, Bobby. I watched you grow from a boy to a man. Every man gets scared, but not all of 'em admit it. It takes strength to say that we need help."

"Bobby," Gary said tenderly, "I want to help. That's why I'm here. That's why all of us are here. I don't want to lose you like I lost your daddy. Will you let us help you?"

I could see Bobby's chest rising and falling as he took in a deep breath and blew it out.

"I gotta smoke," Bobby announced, as he got up and walked to the back porch.

By the time I caught up with him, he'd already lit a cigarette and was sucking heavily on it. Like before, I didn't crowd him or force a conversation. But it was cold, and I'd left my coat inside. I hoped we wouldn't be out here too long.

After Bobby flicked his cigarette off the porch onto the ground below, he turned to me, his eyes bloodshot and streaked like an animal.

"You get your jollies outta doing this?" he said in my direction. "'Cause this is messed up. I'm not even awake."

"I know this is a lot to take in," I told him. "But to answer your question, no, I don't get my jollies from this. I'm not here to judge you. But I lost a lot in my addiction." I went on to tell him some of the details of just how much my addiction stole from me, closing with, "I'll do anything to get you help." Then I added, "If you want that help."

Bobby searched my face for a long moment. Maybe he was deciding whether to lash out at me. Or maybe he wondered if I was telling the truth. Either way, he headed back inside.

Bobby sat back in his spot on the couch. Without speaking, I caught Julia's eye and nodded that it was her time to read.

Slowly, Julia pulled out the notebook and placed it on her lap.

At the same time, I talked to God silently. *Lord, you know that we came to offer hope and redemption for one of your suffering children. Help Julia get through this, and keep Bobby's heart soft to Your leading and her words. Amen.*

CHAPTER TWENTY-SIX

RANDY'S STORY

"Of all the ways to lose a person, death is the kindest."

—RALPH WALDO EMERSON

Like Bobby, I had a strong wife.

When it was time to leave our dream house, Lydia got up early for the movers, bustling about the house, packing up the last odds and ends that we'd left out to use that morning. She shed tears too. But I didn't know at the time, since I never woke up.

Then she came to rouse me from bed.

"Honey," she must have said. "You should get up; the movers will be here soon." But I didn't move.

According to Lydia, she turned frantic, grabbing my shoulders and beating on my chest. "Randy, wake up! Randy, get up NOW!"

Emily and Brady heard her cries and rushed in. They also shook me and screamed at me to wake up.

My body, which had once reacted to the slightest movement

on the field, lay unresponsive. They switched the light on, revealing my grey flesh.

Lydia yanked the phone off the bedside table and dialed 911. Things quickly grew chaotic. Two female EMTs pulled up to the house, strode through the front door, and rushed past my kids. They maneuvered my massive frame out of the bed onto a gurney, carrying me back outside where they slid me into the ambulance.

It was all in a day's work to them, but to my family—numbly on the sidelines, watching it unfold like a series of disjointed snapshots—this scene was other-worldly.

Lydia's mom arrived. As my family observed the ambulance, the landscape of this trauma grew wider, etching itself into their souls.

And it wasn't just family. Neighbors started filing out of their homes, as if it were time to watch the Super Bowl out on the street. Except this former NFL player lay lifeless.

Lydia stayed inside the house with the kids, standing at the window and watching the ambulance from behind the curtains, looking for any confirmation of life or death or anything in between. Her mom prayed aloud and tried to console the kids. That emergency vehicle sat parked in our driveway for ages while everyone watched—waiting.

"Heavenly Father, please bring Randy back," Lydia prayed quietly. I'd like to say she prayed because she loved me and feared that she'd lost me. Truth is, I think she was probably pissed at me. But Lydia always prays, even when she's mad as hell. She's that kind of gal—a true prayer warrior. Did I tell you I married up?

Meanwhile, I also watched this strange scene unfold. Except I wasn't peering out of the window of our soon-to-be abandoned home. I wasn't standing inside that crushed dream, holding onto the last drip of life it still held. I wasn't praying for my life to be saved.

Instead, I was hovering over my body inside the ambulance. From the ceiling of the vehicle, I looked down. I was dead, but I could see my body below on the gurney.

If you want to call bullshit, I get it. If a teammate would have told me something like this back in my playing days, I'd have told him to check his helmet for cracks. But this image played out for me clear as day.

I saw my neighbor standing behind the vehicle, trying to peep through the back window of the ambulance to see what was going on. *Lookie-loo.*

I saw those two EMTs diligently working on my large frame. Their orange medical kit looked like a tackle box. I saw them unlatch the top, as if they were out fishing and looking for the perfect fly. I peered down at all the box's compartments. They meticulously pulled a syringe out of one compartment and tore off the package. They kept watch on my sealed eyes as their arms maneuvered over me—looking for any sign of life.

What I did not see at the time, but recognized only years later, were God's hands also outstretched over the entire scene. *Over my dead body.*

One EMT stood by my feet, wiggling my toes continuously, while the other was at my armpit. The latter took that syringe, filled it with something, and shoved the needle into my chest—plunging its contents deep below my ribcage.

Suddenly, it was like someone jammed my soul back into my body. In one movement, my eyes shot open, I looked up at the EMTs, and I jerked onto my side. I exhaled a roar as I puked like crazy—the most violent nausea ever to hit me. Whatever they'd given me to reverse my overdose turned me inside out. That ambulance was a mess, and I pity the guy who had to clean it.

After the ambulance sped away with me flailing inside, Lydia drove to meet me at the ER.

While I'd seen myself lifeless on the gurney, once my body was revived, I blacked out for the ambulance ride. I was alive but unaware of anything.

But in the hospital, my focus returned. Glancing at the nurses bustling around me, I remembered my family.

The ER doctor assured Lydia I would be okay. Once she heard that immediate danger had passed, she rushed into task mode. I married a strong woman. And it was moving day. And in some sense, she was probably relieved that I couldn't cause any more trouble that day. *Dying was enough for one day.*

"I have to get back home," I told my nurse. "We're moving today, and I can't let my wife do that alone."

"Uh-huh," the nurse said, as she fiddled with my IV. She reminded me of my mom, sweet—and down-to-business. I couldn't tell if she judged me, because she was trained to be kind and professional to everyone.

"Look, I appreciate all you're doing," I said, shifting my tone to sweet-talk mode. "But I feel fine now, thanks to you."

Sensing my bargaining, she appeased me, mustering all the cheer she could for someone nursing an inebriated man back from death. "We'll get you out of here as soon as we can!"

It turned out "soon as we can" did not mean I'd go home that day. I lay there, useless to my wife who was moving our household alone.

Lydia later told me everything that happened while I was unresponsive. My account of that day lined up with what Lydia and witnesses saw: I died and was brought back to life. Unlike Lydia, I felt no emotion as I recalled the life-and-death battle over my body.

But what transpired in my family's hearts remained invisible to me. Anyone around them could see the pain carving deeper grooves with each of my failures, like another flash flood damaging an already-eroded canyon.

The pills that numbed me also blurred my vision to their pain. My own pain was too blinding. All I could do was hold it together long enough to get out of the hospital and hope to land some more pills.

At midnight, as I lay in my bed, I pictured Lydia's stunning face as I fell asleep to the heavy weight of my shame.

But it wasn't until later that I could fully imagine not only the beauty of her physical body, but what she went through that day—and that night. When my doting wife was finally done with the brutal, exhausting move, she walked through our house one final time. I later pictured her gliding in the moonlight beside the pool that had seen our kids grow up—the memories of laughter and love quivering beneath the still, dark water. Only the faint flutter of the moon's reflection could break the deep shadows.

Turning back into the house, down the hallway, past our bedroom, I pictured her pausing to remember the years passing —including the glory and elation, the changes we'd endured, and the pain we'd fought back, again and again.

Continuing past the kids' rooms and into the kitchen, she sighed softly, with no one to witness. Her tall, slight frame alone in the dim light, she soaked a mop with water, slapping it against the cold, tile floor. She would clean up the mess that was left by our lives, washing it clean for someone else.

Starting in one corner, she wrestled her beautiful, exhausted frame against that mop, trying to erase any memory that we'd ever existed. She scrubbed every last footprint away.

But some of the scars and stains couldn't be removed.

She stepped off the floor, lathering the last square foot. As she plunged the mop into the bucket, the filth we'd left behind clouded the water.

I'm guessing most of that filth was mine, and it seemed to be following me—despite how many times others mopped up for me.

Tears began to flow, as she then dumped the last traces of our lives down the sink. She exited and locked the door for the last time, imagining the new family that would soon fill our home with laughter.

CHAPTER TWENTY-SEVEN

THE INTERVENTION

"The only way to tell the truth is to speak with kindness.
Only the words of a loving man can be heard."

—HENRY DAVID THOREAU

December 20, 2018

As I looked at Julia, about to read her letter, I was grateful she'd never seen Bobby the way Lydia had seen me. But I knew if he continued, it could happen. I didn't want that for Bobby, or Julia, or any of those loved ones sitting in front of me. I prayed once more, silently, *God, move in ways only You can do. Only You can save Bobby.*

All eyes were on Julia as she began reading.

Bobby,

You've been part of the three happiest times in my life. I can't believe that it's been ten years since my first happiest day, when I met you at the Christmas party at work. I told my friend on the way home that I'd given you my number, and I said, "He better call me!"

Even before our first date, I called my mom to tell her about you. I felt this instant connection. I even asked her how she knew that Daddy was the one. She said that "you just know." After dating you for three months, I just knew that you were my one.

The second happiest day of my life was when you married me. One of the cutest things about you is that you have no idea how special you are. Any woman would have been thrilled to be with you. But you picked me. I can still feel you sliding the ring on my finger before the preacher declared us married. And my heart pounded when the preacher introduced us as Mr. and Mrs.

You were there on the third happiest day of my life on July 18, 2008, when Anna was born. You were in the room the whole time, and you cried so hard that you didn't even take any pictures. I was crying, too. We had a beautiful child together, and I just knew that we'd be the happiest family. We had your family in town, a gorgeous home, our beautiful little angel, and each other. My life felt complete, and my heart was full of such joy.

As Julia started reading, Lydia moved closer to wrap her arm around Julia's shoulder. Large tears fell from Julia's eyes as she spoke, clouding her vision until she wiped them away. Lydia, too, so full of empathy and having lived through a similar version in our own seemingly all-American family, let large tears fill her eyes without removing them.

Two people in the room had an even harder time containing their emotions. One was Bobby. Without looking at him, I could hear him sobbing quietly. His breath became choppy as emotion poured out. As he wept, a sweet, acidic smell like vinegar filled the room. Between his labored breathing, sweat, and tears, the odor of alcohol became unmistakable.

Like Bobby, I struggled to keep it together while Julia read. The words Julia spoke could have been penned by Lydia, except Lydia might not have included the night we met as one of her top three happiest moments. Yet I knew for sure that the births of Emily and Brady were on the list. Lydia might have added the joy when I signed to play with Tampa Bay, when the entire world seemed in our favor.

What choked me up was knowing where her letter would go next. Even before Julia continued reading, I knew that things didn't remain happy. They hadn't for me.

Julia took a several moments to gain her composure before reading.

But all that changed around the time you wrecked the four-wheeler. And now, you're not part of my joy or life. You've gotten DUIs and can't keep a real job. I know that the accident, two surgeries, and physical therapy weren't what you planned. But I never imagined that you would get hooked on narcotics. Do you know what it's like for me to deal with people who've had accidents caused by drugs and alcohol when I'm scared to death that the next ambulance might bring you in? I've seen so many drug overdoses, and I live with constant fear that you will be one of them. But I can't even talk to you about it. You've gotten so angry with me that I'm afraid. I don't want Anna growing up around that rage.

You told me that you'd get your life together and find a job, and I felt some hope. I was fine with you staying home with Anna while I worked. But you drove our baby without a license while drinking, endangering her, and lying to me. Anna is watching all of this. She knows that things aren't right. She's afraid of you when you drink. She crawls in bed with me to get away from you when you come in late at night.

Bobby lowered his head to his chest. "Are you listening, Bobby?" Grandfather Robert asked from his chair.

When I asked you to leave, I really thought that you hit bottom and would get help for your addiction. Because that's what it is, Bobby. It's not a drinking problem. It's not medication for pain. You have an addiction, and I don't think you can stop on your own. You are not yourself. The man I married loved to work, play, hike with me, garden, go fishing and hunting, and spend time with friends and family. He cried happy tears when his little girl was born, and he promised her that he would never let anything bad happen.

Bobby, I live in a house that I can't afford with a daughter who cries herself to sleep most nights, thinking you left because you don't love her. We're alone because of your addiction.

I want my best friend and husband back. And Anna needs her daddy.

When Julia finished, the only sound was Bobby sobbing. He no longer tried to hold it in. He used his sleeves to wipe away tears and snot.

I moved from behind the couch to stand behind Julia who sat on the coffee table.

"Bobby," I began, "I know that some of this was hard to hear. But I heard something else this morning: a lot of love. Your family, Gary, Lydia, and myself are here to help you get the help you need."

Bobby continued crying, and his head bobbed up and down. Even before Julia began her letter, shame gripped the young man, and he couldn't look anyone in the eye. Gone was the strong, angry façade he showed upon waking. Bobby seemed broken.

"If you're ready, I'll take you to a place where you can get help. I'll even come by the treatment center to check on you."

Bobby wiped his face and shook his head from side to side.

"We can't afford it," he said. "I owe enough money already. And I have to get his truck fixed," he motioned to Teddy.

"The truck can wait," I said as Teddy said, "Don't worry about the truck right now." I was thrilled to hear those words.

"And as far as treatment, that's taken care of," I told him.

I didn't go into detail, but Julia's insurance company would cover up to sixty days of inpatient care.

"I don't want to leave my family," Bobby started.

Before I could say anything, Wilma jumped in with an item from her list of what she would say if Bobby refused to go.

"Well, you'll have to leave, Bobby," she said with the confidence of a supportive group around her. "Because you can't stay in my home if you don't get help. I love you too much to see you dead or hauled off to jail because you hit me again."

This time, Wilma didn't couch her black eye with an excuse like, "It was an accident."

"You're going," she said straightly, "Or you'll have to find someplace else to live."

Bobby sat on the couch and rocked his head slightly forward and back as that sunk in.

"I have court," Bobby protested. "I can't leave the county. And then I'm going to go to jail."

An intervention requires a playbook. But once the intervention starts, it's like what happens just before the ball is snapped in a football game. All bets are off. Sometimes the quarterback calls an audible if he doesn't like what he sees, or he sees a better opportunity when he scans the entire field.

As the center, I had to read the person in my face, snap the ball, and keep the opposing player from laying a hand on my quarterback. But running interventions, I learned how to take in the entire situation and make changes on the fly. All that training taught me how to see things more like a quarterback than a center.

Within minutes of meeting Bobby, I was confident he'd go to treatment. But that didn't mean I didn't need to do my part. Doing my part meant *not screwing it up.* I had to know when to keep my mouth shut. Saying too much can take a person away from their thoughts. Saying too little can give the person time to look for a way out. As the quarterback of this intervention, I had to look for openings and take them.

I hadn't planned on calling this play, but when Bobby brought up court, I had to take advantage of the opportunity.

"The district attorney is willing to delay your court date if you get help right now," I responded. "Go to treatment now, and who knows? Maybe he'll work with you when you come back and face the charges against you. But even if he doesn't, you can't tell me that you're happy right now. It's time to retake charge of your life and face your addiction head-on."

"I don't want to go," Bobby pleaded. "I'll stay here and go to AA or something. I don't need to go anywhere. This is where I belong."

"I have a place for you, Bobby," I offered again. "Your mom has already purchased your plane ticket to Florida. We'll go together. You won't be alone in any of this."

Bobby didn't say anything.

"Don't be a jackass," Robert said from his chair. "This man here is offering your life back. Do you really think you'd be better off living on the streets and finding your next drink in the gutter?"

Sister Allison put her arm around Bobby and hugged him tight.

"It will be alright, Bobby. You can do this," she said kindly, standing up. "I'll help you pack a bag."

Instead of moving, Bobby looked at his wife for the first time that morning.

"I'm..." he started to say something. "Can we work through this?"

Julia looked exhausted, having used what seemed to be all her emotional energy reading her letter.

"If you get some help, we'll see what happens," she said noncommittally. "You know I love and miss you, and all's I wanted was to put our family back together. But if you don't get help, I have to move on. I can't keep waiting for that call that you're dead."

"Why don't you go with Allison and pack some clothes, Bobby," I said as a statement and not a question. "The flight leaves in a few hours, and we got a drive ahead of us."

Bobby nodded. Then he rose and walked with his sister to the room he'd been sleeping in.

After he turned the corner, I addressed the folks in the room.

"I can't tell you how proud I am of all of you," I told them sincerely. "He's going to get help, because you all loved him enough to do this today."

"What happens now?" Wilma asked.

"We will get him all checked in and settled," I responded. "As challenging as it was to get to this point, the real work is still ahead. I tell you that from my own experience. Right now, he's got the willingness to get help and few other options."

"I mean," Wilma asked, "What do *we* do now? Just wait for him to come home? Can we talk to him?"

"Oh, I gotcha," I told her. "A huge part of working the program involves you. You will be part of regular calls while he's there. And you'll be invited to visit for family weekends where you will work with a therapist with Bobby. And that's for you, too, Julia. I would encourage you and Anna to visit if you can. Addicts get better when the entire family works together."

"Did I do a good job shutting up?" Robert asked with a small smile.

"Yes, Robert," I laughed. "Not only were you great at shutting up, but when you talked, you were powerful. You really helped open his eyes."

"Yeah," Robert said. "But I don't have an addiction. I was just a drunk," Robert snorted.

"Call it what you will," I said. "Whatever it is, you quit drinking. And there's no wrong way to do that."

When Allison and Bobby returned, Bobby put an old duffle bag next to the couch.

"Bobby, why don't you say your goodbyes while I take your bag to the car?" I suggested. Catching Lydia's eye, I motioned for her to grab her things. From experience, long and tearful goodbyes can make a person change their mind. My read of the situation was that Bobby still may have been intoxicated enough from the night before to be a little blurry about what was happening. This was not the time to drag things out.

With Lydia on one side and me on the other, the two of us wrapped our arms over Bobby's shoulders as we walked to the car.

"I'm very proud of you, Bobby," Lydia said as she patted him on the back. "You are making the right decision. God will bless you. Just wait and see what He has in store."

Once settled in the car, as I pulled the car onto the road, a little gravel kicked up as I accelerated. Turning the car towards the highway, I could see the first rounded edge of the sun breaking the horizon directly in front of us.

Buckle up, Bobby, I said to myself. *You're going to be okay, but that doesn't mean you aren't in for a rough ride.*

CHAPTER TWENTY-EIGHT

RANDY'S STORY

"I don't know where I am going, but I am on my way."

—Voltaire

By the time I was released two days after my overdose, Lydia, with the help of family and friends, had us completely moved into our next home—no thanks to me.

Like Bobby, my secret finally lay in plain sight, and I could no longer hide that I was a drug addict. Unlike Bobby, I was not ready to change that status. Instead, I'd just have to learn *how not to die.*

The years folded into each other. Emily finished high school in 2002. Brady was still at home playing football. I held things together in some sense, meaning I didn't have another overdose. But I kept using.

Moving from our dream house didn't solve our financial problems; rather, it delayed them. It meant when I'd get blitzed out of my mind, I'd stumble into a much smaller house.

I isolated myself from anyone healthy. My new team and community became the doctors who gave me drugs—or the dealers I hit up. Instead of following a playbook developed by strong coaches, I wrote my own. But my playbook wasn't about winning anything; it was about how to stay stoned out of my mind while staying alive.

The more drugs I did, the more my shame buried me. I couldn't begin to look at what I was doing to my family. Feeling like the biggest hypocrite in the world, I stopped teaching in church. If I showed up on Sundays, I fell asleep in the pew.

More time passed in a blur. Lydia worked tirelessly to get me help by way of hospitalizations and treatment centers. Sometimes I'd stay a couple of days, but then I'd check myself out. You can't help someone who doesn't want it. And clearly, I didn't want help as much as I wanted drugs.

Once, Lydia took me to a doctor we knew to help get me off the drugs.

"Hand me the pills," he said, rattling off a protocol to taper me off that involved Lydia doling me my pills each day.

So I went through the motions. I went to Lydia each day like a child, and she handed me my daily dose. Then I'd walk away, and a few hours later, I'd take the pills I'd managed to scour behind her back.

As I rode the rollercoaster that had become my life, I'd ascend from manipulative drug abuser who would take grocery money to get high, to pragmatic husband and father who knew that I couldn't afford drugs and a family. The effort to scrounge up enough money to buy drugs became exhausting. We didn't have the funds to sustain my habit. I'd pay $300 to see a doctor and another $350 for pills. Those visits got more frequent, which meant we never had money.

Finally, worn out from shame and fatigued from chasing drugs, I decided to try quitting cold turkey. But my "seizure disorder" returned with a vengeance. I never felt the seizures coming on. They would hit me, dropping me to the floor instantly. As I writhed, I'd bite my tongue, shake, and scream like a madman. These seizures could last up to ten minutes, and during the worst attacks, I'd knock over chairs or anything else that got in my way.

Once they passed, I could talk, but not right away. And then my voice didn't sound right, and my body felt off center.

Even as I managed to keep my job and work my way up in the company, we stayed broke. I didn't have a money problem. I had a drug problem. Whatever we earned, I spent on drugs. But I *had to*, I told myself. I had to keep the seizures at bay. So once I'd spent every penny we'd earned, I started hitting up loan shops. I'd go a couple times a week to get enough to cover pills.

One day, Lydia pulled into the grocery store parking lot and saw my car. She walked up to the window and knocked on the window. I was asleep, slumped over in my seat. She called it a God thing, but at the time, I just found it annoying. Either way, she helped me get home before anyone could call the police.

The shame and guilt didn't change my behavior. If anything, they made me more desperate to feel nothing. But with no credit, no cash, no more dealers extending me handouts, and no prospects of earning extra money, my access to drugs became more threatened. Not willing to face my pain without my dear friends, opioids and benzos, I found a new funding source. I started pawning away my life.

At first, I sold things no one cared much about. Then I moved into my own personal stuff.

One day, a friend called Lydia. "Hey, I think Randy's Baylor Southwest Conference ring is on e-Bay." Lydia didn't notice that ring missing, because I'd kept it in a drawer and never wore it.

Then I pawned a beautiful antique clock Dad had rebuilt, ignoring the knowledge that he'd lovingly restored it with his own hands for a year to get it back in its original state. Walking into the pawn shop to exchange his hard work for drug money triggered my darkest emotions, but I allowed myself some solace, knowing that I'd soon have enough money to numb my pain for a few more hours.

Finally, I hawked my ring from the NFL Players Association, commemorating the ten years I'd played in the league.

Desperation has no morals. I was robbing Peter to pay Paul. Eventually, I pawned everything of value that I owned, while at the same time my need for drugs increased.

I pawned all of Lydia's gold chains and diamonds, jewelry I'd given her through the years.

I pawned a ring my dad had given Lydia that she absolutely cherished. She found my pawn shop receipt and bought the ring back.

Next, I took my son's rifle from under his bed and pawned it. When he noticed it missing, he and his mom found the receipt and knew where to find it. They drove to the pawn shop and bought it back.

When I sold my wife's beloved ring a second time, she couldn't afford to buy it back again. It was gone forever.

A guy who'd once made enough money to buy one of the nicest houses in Houston was now scrounging up his kid's stuff and hauling it to shady shops in parts of town no one wanted to visit.

You might wonder if Lydia ever considered leaving me during those years. Yes and no. No one could put up with the things I'd done, some of which I can't even stomach writing about here in my own words. I did things no man should ever do when he loves his wife. So of course she wanted me out of her life.

But as much as she grieved over my life, God wouldn't let her leave me. He whispered to her heart: "I want to heal Randy. I want to *restore* your family." And that is what Lydia held onto and desired with her deepest being, even when everyone told her she was crazy. Lydia believed in God's power to restore me —and us.

Her faith in God gave her a reason to hold on.

Brady became a senior in high school. Lydia didn't want to disrupt things for the kids.

But *apparently,* I tested her. I say *apparently,* because I was often in a blackout when I did.

I did many things in a state of *apparently.* And the things I did in my addiction knew no bounds.

I got home one night and saw dents all over the front of my truck. *Apparently,* I'd wrecked on the way home. More than once, I'd run into guardrails or hit another car pulling out of a parking lot.

Another time, I had a seizure as I climbed out the pool while home by myself. If it had been just a second earlier, I'd have seized in the pool. The headlines would have read, "Randy Grimes Dead of *Apparent* Drowning."

One day, Emily found me in the driveway, passed out with my foot on the gas. *Apparently,* by some miracle, I'd gotten the truck in park before going out cold. Lydia came out of the house and switched off the ignition. She told me the hood was so hot you could fry an egg on it.

It got to the point when Emily or Brady would have friends over, they would find out where I happened to be in the house so they could walk their friends as far away from me as possible to avoid seeing me passed out. *Shame.*

Repeatedly, my family tried to confront me about my drug abuse, but it usually led to Lydia screaming and pleading, and Emily crying. When words failed, Lydia would dig through my shoes or every pocket in every clothing item in the closet looking for my stash. If she'd find it, she'd throw the pills at me or flush them.

My seizures were so common that my family didn't react. They just went through the motions. Both of my kids found me passed out or having seizures on such a regular basis, they would talk casually with the EMTs on the street who were hauling their daddy away.

The hallucinations began getting more frequent.

And still, I kept popping pills.

I preferred doctors over drug dealers, not because I was following the law—but because the street drugs were more expensive.

One time, Lydia found the number of one of my dealers. She wasted no time trying to shut him down.

"Don't you ever sell drugs to my husband again!" she yelled over the phone. "Do you hear me? I'll call the police if you do it again!" Did I tell you she's Texan? Just like a perfect barbecue sauce, Lydia's always been a masterful blend of fire and honey.

Great things happened throughout this time, not that I knew much about them. Emily graduated from Texas A&M in 2006 and got engaged. Lydia became consumed with helping Emily plan her wedding. Lydia and her parents scraped together every cent to throw Emily the perfect wedding. Lydia's parents paid for most of it. It was a stunning ceremony, or so I'm told. My body was there, but my shame was so great, my mind and heart were obliterated by a dense fog.

My so-called life continued with an increasing series of blackouts, detox centers, seizures, and drug treatment.

You might wonder why the treatment didn't stick for me. I gained tools. However, my physical pain became endless. After leaving detox, I told myself that I'd done everything within my power to be rid of drugs, but I couldn't sleep. I lived in pain. And that's when I'd convince myself that I could do drugs right this time. I'd take them *as prescribed.*

And of course, my resolve would last a day, before I'd be right back to abusing as much or even more than I had before.

As my addiction squeezed the life from me, so did my stress. Lydia kept telling me I needed to hit rock bottom, but I honestly didn't think I could fall much further. In 2007, I lost another job. I'd failed to offer any financial or emotional support for Emily's wedding, and now she and her husband were expecting their first baby. As much as I'd let down my kids, I couldn't imagine turning into a good grandpa. I couldn't afford Brady's tuition, so we took out another huge loan for Texas A&M. Thank God my brother Dickey and sister Roxanne helped pay for Brady's truck and rent. And our children always worked during high school and college. They knew they had to help. They never complained and always had excellent grades.

Having nothing left to lose and believing I must finally be at my bottom, I tried treatment again.

I went right into detox at the facility. But it was done too quickly, and I started hallucinating. The center sent me to Methodist Hospital, because it was bigger and more able to deal with my brand of insanity.

By the time my family arrived at the ER, my hallucinations were so violent that it took ten people to hold me down.

I am driving on a roundabout while another car is chasing me. I keep going around and around, but that car is staying on my tail and gaining ground on me. It keeps getting closer and closer.

I was terrified of this hallucination, which was happening in real-time in the ER. Lydia tells me I kept saying something about the "beautiful birds." I don't remember any birds in my delusions, but I vividly recall the endless circle of hell I drove around in that horrible roundabout.

Brady tried to hold me down, while the hospital staff called in more nurses. I looked at him blankly.

"Who this guy?" I asked, terrified and on guard, "And why does he want to mess with me?" Later, I learned that when I didn't recognize my son, it broke his heart. And thinking back on it breaks mine.

Finally, they got a shot into me. Once I zoned out, they tied me to my bed and put me in the ICU. For three days, I hovered between life and death. I remember nothing. I'm told that my brother and sister came to see me, just in case it was the last time.

The medical professionals kept me in the psych area for three weeks. Lydia thought I was going through some kind of rehab. There were psychologists and therapists talking to me, but again, nothing took hold for long.

As my mind settled and returned, I again relied on my charm offensive—climbing the rollercoaster into the light.

It worked, and they released me.

Within a few days, I went right back to using, plummeting and twisting into the dark. My life was becoming a ride I wasn't sure I'd survive.

CHAPTER TWENTY-NINE

THE INTERVENTION

"The key to growth is acknowledging your fear of the unknown and jumping in anyway."

—Jen Sincero

December 20, 2018

I married well. Even after all of these years, Lydia's voice brings music to my ears. This is especially true when we work together. During interventions, I'm hyper-focused, like when playing football. But after an intervention, like after a gridiron battle, I'm exhausted and need to unplug.

That's where Lydia shines. Not only does she love on families, but when she's on the road with me, she talks to our passenger, while I just keep my ears on the GPS.

We learned early on when working together that while I drove, she should sit in the backseat with our passenger. Once, when we were taking a man to treatment, he slipped a bottle of liquor from his bag and was just about ready to knock it back when we noticed. Another time, even with Lydia in the backseat, a girl tried to swallow a handful of pills. Lydia stopped her.

While I drove, Lydia watched Bobby—without *actually* watching, you know? She followed his energy, talking when he talked, and sat in silence when he looked out the window.

"So where is this treatment center?" Bobby asked with his eyes forward.

"It's in Florida, near West Palm Beach," Lydia answered. "We'll fly into Fort Lauderdale, then someone will take you the rest of the way. Have you ever been to Florida?" She directed the conversation.

"I went to Fort Lauderdale on spring break once," Bobby responded.

"Did you just love the ocean?" Lydia asked, showing her own excitement.

"Yeah, it was nice," Bobby answered without much enthusiasm. "I went with friends. I don't remember much, but I know I went back to school sunburned."

They kept talking like this while I drove. I listened, and I learned some other interesting things about his life.

Bobby told Lydia that if he and Julia didn't get back together, Anna might be Wilma's only grandchild. After trying for years, Allison and Teddy went to a fertility doctor. They couldn't have children without in vitro fertilization.

Bobby also mentioned that his mom had dated a man when he and Allison were both away in college. Apparently, Wilma stopped seeing him because he drank all the time.

After what seemed like a long drive, I pulled into the rental car return area. I thought about dropping Lydia and Bobby off at departures, but I didn't want Lydia to shoulder the entire responsibility of keeping an eye on Bobby. It took forever to drop off the car, get on the shuttle, and get checked in for our flights.

Before we headed to security, Bobby asked if he could step

outside to smoke. Checking the time, I knew that we still had nearly three hours before our flight. I didn't want Bobby jonesing for a smoke during the wait, so I agreed, and we stepped outside while Lydia held our spot at the security checkpoint.

Once Bobby lit a cigarette, he wanted to talk.

"Were you telling the truth about you having a problem with drugs?"

"I sure was," I nodded. "I started taking pain pills and benzos when I played football."

"You played football? Where?" he asked.

"I played center for the Tampa Bay Buccaneers for ten years," I answered. "I took a lot of hits and had constant pain. So I justified taking pills so I could sleep and play."

"You took drugs *while playing*?" he asked. "Don't they do drug testing in sports?"

"Yes, especially now," I told him. "But I started playing thirty years ago. Back then, the team doctors and trainers would hand out pain meds like candy. What started during football then continued for around twenty years, as I shopped for doctors to write prescriptions for me."

"But you seem like you're doing alright now. So did you go to treatment, too?" he asked.

"I sure did," I nodded. "I took everything I learned in football into treatment. I memorized the playbook, surrounded myself with strong players, listened to my coaches, and did whatever they told me."

"Julia told me that I wouldn't get better until I hit bottom," Bobby said. "Did you?"

"Yes. And hitting bottom hurts," I told him with empathy.

He put out his cigarette. While walking back inside, he put more questions to me.

"So you don't drink at all now? And you don't take any pills?"

"Nothing," I said. "I don't even like to take cold medicine. I don't want to let any part of my old insanity back in my life."

"But don't you miss it?" he pushed.

"That's like asking if I miss wrecking cars."

When I said that about cars, Bobby looked at me.

"Yeah, I wrecked a big ol' work truck. Drove it into a lake, of all things," I said. "I wouldn't be alive if I hadn't surrendered my life and will over to God by entering recovery."

We saw Lydia in the security line and moved to join her. Given the Christmas holiday, the airport was a madhouse. Heck, even if it weren't the holiday, Hartsfield-Jackson Atlanta International Airport is the busiest airport in the world. So it wasn't a surprise that security looked like the line for the most popular Disney World rides.

As you might imagine, Bobby and I absorbed quite a few angry looks as we squeezed past others to join Lydia.

"I'm just joining my wife right there," I kept saying.

Once together, Bobby said, "I don't want to go to treatment, but I've tried quitting on my own. It never works. I can't stop puking when I go cold turkey."

"I get it," I said. "When I tried to stop, I had seizures and blackouts."

"A four-wheeler fell on me right before Anna was born," Bobby shared, likely not remembering all that had been shared in family letters a few hours earlier.

"Shoulder pain?" I asked, encouraging him to keep talking.

"Yeah," he nodded. "I couldn't rotate my right arm at all. When I tried, it felt like a knife puncturing me. I had surgery twice and then physical therapy so I could move it. But it still hurts. The doctor kept telling me to take Advil and Tylenol, but that didn't do squat. Finally, he gave me a muscle relaxer and Percocet to help me sleep."

I nodded without interrupting.

"But when I ran out of Percocet, the pain came back even worse." Bobby started to reveal more.

"Did you take Percocet with a beer chaser?" I asked flatly.

"Jack Daniels," he nodded. "I started to drink more to block out pain. Then I found another doctor who believed that I was still hurting and wrote me another prescription."

"Do you still have a prescription?" I asked, trying to figure out what chemicals were in his body that might need detoxing.

"Yes and no," Bobby said. "I had one for a while. But now I get them from a friend. Well, just someone I met in class when I got my first DUI."

"Are you still taking Percocet?" I followed up.

"Sometimes," he shrugged.

"Do you have any on you now?" I continued.

"I got a few in my bag," he said, pointing to his duffle.

"Why don't you show me?" I asked.

While Bobby and I talked, Lydia stood watching and listening quietly. Lydia knew intuitively when to jump in and when to sit back.

Bobby rummaged through his bag for a couple of minutes. When he couldn't find it, his face took on a panicked look. Then his fingers landed on the bottle that had slid to the bottom. He stood back up, holding the bottle between his thumb and index finger of his right hand.

The bottle looked to be half full. During my days of popping pills, I would've considered that bottle half-empty. And that would have put me in a frenzy to get more.

He handed me the bottle.

The prescription was a couple of years old. I poured a few into my hands, recognizing OxyContin and Percocet, the latter being Oxycodone mixed with acetaminophen, like what's found in Tylenol. I saw a couple of Xanax and at least one Vicodin in the bottle. I held up a pill I didn't recognize.

"What's this?" I asked.

"I don't know," Bobby shrugged. "I don't remember where I got that one."

"Tell you what," I told him as I put the pills back in the bottle. "Why don't I hold onto these," choosing words that formed a statement instead of a question.

Bobby's face changed quickly.

"No," he said with a look of fear on his face. "I need those for pain. I'll just take one when I need it."

"These aren't prescribed to you. You don't even know if these are legitimate pharmaceutical-grade medicines, or if they are something made in some guy's basement that's stamped to look real."

"No, no," Bobby shook his head. "I've been taking those for a long time. They're real. And safe. Hand them back now," he held out his hand. "Shit," he shook his head, reprimanding himself, "I shouldn't have said anything."

"You did the right thing." I gave his shoulder a light squeeze. "The TSA or airport police don't have any problem with me carrying these. They all know me. But they don't know you. I don't want them getting the local police involved." I lowered my voice to stress the seriousness.

Of course, I wasn't exactly telling the truth. Being an interventionist doesn't permit me to transport narcotics. And neither the TSA nor the airport police know me from Adam. And actually, people carry medication on planes all the time. They aren't looking for Granny carrying blood pressure medicine. They're trying to prevent drug mules from smuggling large quantities hidden in checked or carry-on bags, or even in the soles of shoes, belts, and things like that. So the truth is that neither Bobby nor I would raise an eyebrow carrying a small bottle of medicine. But I didn't want Bobby to have those drugs. He was my responsibility now, and I intended to get him help without stopping in the ER for an overdose.

Bobby was not happy. And I understood. Many alcoholics

hide bottles of booze around the house for any "emergency" that might arise. I brought one woman into treatment who had replaced the contents of her shampoo bottle with vodka, so she could mix herself a little Pantene Cocktail after check-in.

"Fine," he said, spitting out the word with tension.

We moved through security, silently making our way to our gate, where we couldn't find three seats together. Heck, we couldn't find two. I offered Bobby the first open seat, while Lydia and I stood.

"Are you hungry?" Lydia asked me. "Why don't I grab us all some food?" she offered.

She found out what Bobby and I wanted and disappeared into the crowded terminal.

"Hey," Bobby said as he stood, "I gotta use the bathroom. Can you watch my bag?"

"Um," I started. Looking at the crowd and the two bags in front of my feet plus my backpack, I didn't see how I could go with him.

"You already have my pills," Bobby said. "I'll just be right in there," he pointed at an overhead sign. "I'll be back in a few minutes."

I shrugged, feeling trapped and torn. Plopping down in the seat Bobby vacated, I pulled our bags to my feet and waited.

It took me a couple of minutes to realize that something was wrong.

CHAPTER THIRTY

RANDY'S STORY

"I prayed that God would open the doors of Heaven and let me in. Instead, he opened the doors of Hell and let me out."

—Randy Grimes

As my addiction chained me to a life that wasn't mine, I'd lie in bed hearing voices on the other side of the wall. Those voices were so real, they filled me with terror. I didn't know what they were saying, but I knew they were talking about what they'd do to me. Taunted, I'd get out of bed, grab a shotgun, load it, and put it next to my bed.

No demons will take me without a fight, I reasoned.

At dinner one evening, I hit Lydia in the leg with a plate of spaghetti. I was hallucinating again. *Apparently,* while I didn't mean to hurt her, I became increasingly violent when I felt the darkness closing on me. At bedtime, Lydia slept in a separate room with her door locked and her purse and keys in her bed. She didn't trust what I might do while hallucinating.

At one point, I disappeared during lunchtime. In a panic, Lydia and her dad drove around looking for me. Finding my truck in front of a 7-11, she ran inside the store. There, I stood off to the side in a dark suit and tie, peering from behind tinted glasses.

"Honey," she said, "What are you doing?"

"Shhhh," I motioned with a finger over my lips. "I'm working."

"Doing what?" she asked as she looked around the store.

"Protecting Malia and Sasha," I answered.

In my hallucination, you see, I was the bodyguard for President Obama's daughters. If the girls wanted a Slurpee, how could I say no?

Lydia and her dad wrangled me into the car and took me to her parents' house, where they could watch me while she returned to work. On the couch, I looked around and saw the fuselage and fellow passengers with me on Air Force One. Malia and Sasha sat quietly next to me. My delusion started to clear a little, but not enough to prevent me from asking Brady to take me to Walmart. "I need to be there when Obama's helicopter touches down in the parking lot," I said.

But Brady wasn't even there. I just thought he was.

During that hallucination, I didn't know who Lydia was. Scared, I pushed her for the first and only time in our marriage.

Lydia lit up the phone, calling every treatment center she could find listed. She heard the same story each time: *no insurance, no treatment.*

Finally, she called the county. They sent someone out.

"I'm fine!" I said when the sheriff arrived. I didn't get admitted anywhere.

I had no direction, no purpose, no self-esteem, and no money. Even with just Lydia and me, we struggled to keep things together. The only items we had of value were our car and house. Or so I thought. One morning, in full sight of the entire neighborhood, a wrecker towed away my car. *Apparently,* when you stop making payments on your car, it's no longer *your* car.

I needed a way to get around, so my mom bought me a Chevy Impala. When Hurricane Ike hit Houston in September of 2008, a tree hit my car. With the insurance money in my hands, I felt like I'd won the lottery. I immediately spent most of that check on pills. With what was left, I bought a beat-up, crappy Range Rover.

We were behind on our mortgage payments too. This house would be the next to go. Instead of waiting for foreclosure, we decided to sell. We wouldn't make a penny, but we wouldn't lose anything, either. We thought we had a buyer, so we moved all our belongings into storage. But the buyer backed out. So while we weren't homeless yet, it was just a matter of time.

For now, we still had a house, just not a stick of furniture.

It was December 2008, Christmas season. We had no bed, no tree, and no presents.

"Randy, I can't sleep here," Lydia said. "The floor is so hard that I'll never get to sleep. I have to work in the morning. Let's go stay with my parents," she insisted.

Lydia's dad had paid for my daughter's wedding. *And now I'm going to sleep under his roof?* I thought. *No.* My shame was deep, and even though I doubted I could get any lower, I just couldn't. I hated to look at myself in the mirror, and there was no way I could take more charity from a man who'd already sacrificed so much for me.

Lydia stayed at her parents' house, probably sleeping in a feather bed, while I continued to squat on the hardwood floors of my own empty house. I guess you could say that we had finally separated, although she hadn't left me for good.

In January of 2009, we got a call from a lady from New Jersey who saw our house online, and she wanted it. Days before, we'd gotten a letter from the bank telling us they were foreclosing the next week. If we could complete the sale in the next few days, we could avoid foreclosure and keep our low credit from reaching a new depth.

"It's a God thing," Lydia gushed, overjoyed. "And it all comes together around God's perfect timing." Looking back on it, I can see that. But at the time, I was barely living.

While the new buyer finished paperwork on her end, Lydia brought me meals each day to keep me alive.

Once the house sold, I became truly homeless instead of just furniture-less. I could fit everything I owned into the rear end of the Range Rover. By that time, I didn't have much left besides some work clothes and papers.

Once my mom learned about this, she helped me again—this time renting a room for me in an extended stay hotel.

Desperate for work—not to provide for my family, but to afford drugs—I took a job at a silk-screening T-shirt company.

I somehow got used to living with frequent seizures and hallucinations. I tolerated living alone out of my car and crashing in some lifeless hotel.

All of that—and my life—was about to change.

Out of the blue, I got a call that my friend had died of an overdose. This buddy and I played together in Tampa. During flights home after games, he was one of those who collected pills with me from the other players. Like me, he medicated his injuries, adding large amounts of alcohol on top of the pills.

We stayed in touch after our playing days. After his death, a brain scan found he had chronic traumatic encephalopathy, usually shortened to CTE. The scan found that he had damage to his frontal lobe. I've known other guys with CTE, and I knew that it could mess with a person's ability to think and reason. Research suggests it can lead to a lot of disease and earlier death.

It turns out a lot of guys who play pro ball have dealt with this. Some of the ones I've met can't even complete a sentence. His wife had become an advocate for increasing awareness about CTE, and she crusaded to get the NFL to be more proactive in preventing and addressing this risk.

There is no way, I thought to myself, thinking back to the young, strong, healthy person I remembered walking out of One Buc Place with me after a grueling training. *There is no way he could be gone. He was so strong.*

I was shocked that this man, a peer and friend, could go to bed one night and never wake up. He was only in his mid-forties, with a beautiful family and several thriving restaurants in Florida.

For the first time since I'd left the NFL, I started to wake up.

I'd suffered twenty documented concussions, not just in the NFL, but all the way back to high school. *Apparently,* I'd come home after practice or a game, plop down on the couch, and stare off into the distance for long periods of time. My mom told me this later.

Mike Singletary, a man called "The Heart of the Defense" when he played with the Super Bowl Champion Chicago Bears in the eighties, and a Pro Football Hall of Famer, broke four helmets against guys throughout his career. He lowered his head and hit men so hard that he shattered those helmets right down the middle. And he broke two of them against my head. At Baylor, I blocked against that guy every day in practice, and he never did anything half speed.

We didn't use brain scans back then. The only concussion test we had was a coach holding up fingers.

"How many fingers?" he'd ask. If you got close, he'd send you back in.

I got hit so hard in one play against the Lions that after stumbling around for a few moments, I sat on their bench.

"How many fingers am I holding up?" my coach asked me after the Lions' coach had sent me back to my team.

"Five?" I answered.

"Close enough. Get back in the game," my coach said.

I got knocked so stupid, I couldn't remember the plays, and I would have to ask teammates near the line of scrimmage before snapping the ball. We constantly helped one another in the huddle, because on any given play, someone had gotten his bell rung. We helped each other stay in the game. No game, no job security. We were a community on the field.

And now one of my brothers was gone.

If God had been in the timing of our house selling, He was just warming up for what came next.

Unknown by me, Lydia had reached out to Gridiron Greats for help. The woman she talked to, Jen Smith, took my name to a group of doctors who helped retired players. The group was called PAST, and they wanted to help me. The woman asked for one thing in return: my permission to be part of a documentary about drug use. *Apparently,* as much I tried to hide it, my addiction was an open secret.

"If you're willing to do this, we'll do two things for you. First, we'll pay for the knee surgery you need," she told me. "Second, we'll get you into treatment."

I'd finally hit rock bottom. I had no options. And for the first time in a long while, I didn't want to end up dead, like my buddy.

"Where exactly is this treatment center?" I asked.

"Florida," she responded.

Florida sounded pretty good to me. Having no reason to say no, I said yes.

I was willing to try.

CHAPTER THIRTY-ONE

THE INTERVENTION

*"If you're brave enough to say goodbye, life will reward you
with a new hello."*

—PAULO COELHO

December 20, 2018

As soon as Bobby left, I pulled out my phone and called Lydia.

"He went to the can," I told her.

"Oh," she said. "I'm in line. Do you want me to come back?"

"How much longer you think you'll be?"

"Not long," she said as she stretched out the last word.
"Maybe five minutes?"

"Just stay there then." I looked around at the standing-
room-only mass of people around me. "I'm gonna grab our stuff
and go after him."

Following the signs to the closest bathroom, I entered the
men's room. Two men stood in line for a stall, but traffic around
the urinal flowed quickly (pun intended). I felt more than a
little awkward, not sure if I should call out Bobby's name. I

knew that would be the fastest way to locate him—that is, if he even was there and willing to be found. But it would also generate glances from onlookers wondering: *Who is Bobby? And what will you do with him when you find him, big guy?*

Either way, I decided against hollering out his name. Instead, I waited outside. After five more minutes, Bobby came out. But instead of heading back to our gate, he walked straight towards a bar and grill across the aisle.

I slid up beside him.

"Looks like you overshot our gate, Bobby," I deadpanned.

"Hey! You know, I was thinking maybe I could pop in there and have just one quick drink. For old time's sake?" he asked, almost comically.

That desire to have one last hurrah before going to treatment is common. It's like knowing you plan to start a diet tomorrow, so you'll just finish all the chips and ice cream in the house to get them out of your system.

One man I took to treatment told me he needed the bathroom. But once inside the stall, he plunged a needle into his neck to use up the remainder of his heroin. He came out of the bathroom and plopped down next to me, completely oblivious to the fountain of blood spurting from his neck.

"Let's just get back to our gate, okay?" I asked Bobby as more of a statement.

I don't have the authority to drag anyone on a plane against his will. At any time, a person can say, "Screw it. I'm not going!" if I push too hard. At the same time, I'm liable for this individual, maybe not legally, but I feel a moral obligation to the person and his family to make sure he's safe until I can deliver him to treatment.

When we got back to our seats, we found Lydia and ate in silence. When it came time to board, I switched Lydia's seat assignment out for Bobby's. Lydia and I had seats together. Since Bobby got one of the last seats on the plane, he was way in the back of the plane in a middle seat. Figuring if he had the opportunity, Bobby would continue to drink, I asked Lydia if she wouldn't mind sitting in Bobby's seat.

Before takeoff, I texted Lydia telling her to have a flight attendant wake me if I happened to fall asleep and "anyone" started drinking. After I sent it, I looked at it again and laughed at myself. I typed "anyone" instead of Bobby's name in case he saw her text. I'm sure he never could have broken my secret code had he seen it.

Fortunately, by the time the flight took off, Bobby started to drop. A combination of being dragged out of bed after a night of drinking, and the long drive, and his head didn't pop up again until the plane touched down. And for that I was grateful. I needed to rest my eyes, too.

By the time we regrouped outside the plane after the flight, I called Travis, a counselor who helped people work through some of the issues that led to their addictions. I updated Travis on the flight and got confirmation that Bobby's transport, Eric, would be arriving soon. "And Bobby had pills on him, by the way, which we now have. I'll give them to Eric."

"Good to know. I've completed as much of Bobby's intake as I could with his wife," Travis said. "But we have some big holes in his usage history. From what you see, do you think he's going to need detox?"

Many treatment facilities have detox centers, because the work of starting recovery can't begin until the withdrawal symptoms have passed. People trying to detox without medical supervision can die. So Travis's question is not one I could even begin to answer.

Not everyone needs detox. It depends on what someone has used and for how long. Over time, the human body builds up a tolerance to the poisons in alcohol or narcotics and craves more to get the same high or relief.

As I detoxed off benzos and pain pills, I felt like death—like

I had a terrible flu tearing apart my insides. On top of that, I had seizures, and my anxiety skyrocketed.

If this is what recovery feels like, I want nothing to do with it, I told myself at my lowest point.

Fortunately though, after five or six days, I started to feel almost human again. Alcohol withdrawal can actually be worse than detoxing from drugs. Many alcoholics go through alcohol withdrawal syndrome, known as AWS. As the name suggests, you don't go through withdrawal while drinking. But hours or even days after a person stops, he may experience serious psychological and physical trauma. AWS can cause the shakes, increased anxiety, headaches, sweats, vomiting, and other hellish feelings. A small number of people go through DTs, delirium tremens, which can be deadly.

"He described some pretty serious withdrawal symptoms when he's tried to go cold turkey," I told Travis. "So probably."

"We'll keep a close eye on him," Travis promised. "I'll update you in a couple of days," he offered.

By the time we got outside after getting our bags, Eric texted to say he was waiting for us. Once we got to the curb, Eric jumped out to greet us.

"Hey, Brother!" Eric said with a big smile.

Eric looked like a huge Midwestern farm boy, one with flaming red hair and arms covered in tattoos. He and I had been in treatment together. At first, I hated him, because he smiled all the time. But once I experienced my own spiritual awakening, that all changed. Eric and I became close friends. Even though I had twenty-five years on him, Eric felt like a brother. After graduating from the program, Eric continued going to meetings and staying plugged into recovery. After he reached one year of sobriety, he took a job with a treatment center, offering to be a driver or anything else they needed. Since then, Eric started taking college classes with hopes of becoming a fully credentialed therapist.

Eric gave me a big hug, then greeted Lydia the same way.

"You must be Bobby, right?" he said, extending a hand to our charge.

Bobby nodded and shook Eric's offered hand.

"I am very pleased to meet you, Bobby," Eric said with a warm grin. "One thing I love about our treatment center is that almost all of us working were once in treatment ourselves. We are proof that *it works if you work it sober*," he said, throwing in a little saying that I'd heard and said thousands of times myself.

"Well, my friend," I said to Bobby, "I leave you in good hands."

"Wait, what?" Bobby asked, a confused look on his face. "I thought you were coming with me."

"Lydia and I have to get going, but trust me: you'll see me again very soon," I promised.

Less than eight hours ago, Bobby had never laid eyes on me before. And in a very short time, he started to look at me as his new security blanket, someone to speak the truth to him and guide him.

That's what makes my role challenging. I want to stay close to every one of these folks I help. Instead, I just lead them to the door of treatment; then I must let go to help the next person. What allows me to let go is that I know I'm taking them somewhere they won't need a security blanket. They will learn how to *let go and let God work His miracle*.

Bobby stood a little stiff as I offered him a hug, but he eventually hugged me back. Then Lydia joined in and hugged Bobby, too. The three of us stood there for a moment. As we let go, Lydia looked Bobby in the eyes and told him, "I'm so glad you're here. I want you to know that I'm going to pray for you every morning for the next thirty days. And I'm going to pray that you and Julia come out on the other side of it stronger than you've ever been, okay?" I knew Lydia meant every word.

Bobby nodded, and I saw tears in his eyes.

"Thanks," he said softly.

"Okay, buddy," Eric said loudly as he clapped his hands together. "We gotta go before the traffic police give us the brush-off."

He grabbed Bobby's bag and put it in the back. Then he came around to me as Bobby sat in the front.

"Travis said you have something for me to dispose of?" Eric asked with his hand out.

"Crud, I almost forgot," I said as I patted down my pockets to locate Bobby's pill bottle.

I handed Eric the pills and hugged him again.

"Bye, Eric," Lydia waved as he jumped in the driver's seat.

While the van pulled away, Lydia put her arm around my back, squeezing my side with her hand.

"Heavenly Father, please be with Bobby and his entire family. It won't be easy for them. But You led us to him for a reason. Thank You for letting us be part of his coming transformation. Let him experience Your love firsthand as his body purges itself of poisons. Stay close to him, and help us know how to best love him. In Jesus's name we pray, Amen."

"Amen," I echoed.

"Randy, you did a great job with Bobby and his family," Lydia told me as she looked up in my eyes.

"So did you, Babe." I leaned down to kiss her head. "You're such a natural."

"Let's go home," Lydia said.

I needed no convincing, as I held onto this moment with tremendous gratitude for all that I had to go home to.

CHAPTER THIRTY-TWO

RANDY'S STORY

"Freedom is realizing you have a choice."

—T.F. HODGE

On September 21, 2009, the film crew and my escort flew into Houston to take me back to Florida for treatment. They started filming me immediately. They even gave me a video camera and asked me to film myself during the process. For the next ninety days, I had cameras intermittently focused on my actions, even as we flew to Florida the next day.

That next morning when I traveled from Texas to Florida to enter treatment, I put on sherbet-orange Columbia fishing shirt and shorts, Top Siders, and socks. I guess I wanted to look as good as I could, or maybe those were my only clean clothes.

I abandoned my ragged Range Rover at the airport in Houston. Flying into Fort Lauderdale, I saw the turquoise water temporarily before we veered inland.

Once in the airport, my constant-companion and escort from the film company led me to wait for the car service that would take us to the treatment center.

I wasn't allowed to take any pills on the plane, and I was getting sick.

This is it, I told myself, standing on that curb, swaying from the nausea and heat. I asked my escort for the last remaining pills I owned. She handed me my bottle.

I poured those fifteen pills into my open palm and stared at them.

I don't need to do this, a small voice whispered inside my head.

Shut the hell up and take the damn pills, another more forceful voice demanded.

I popped them all in my mouth, held them for a moment, then swallowed.

The crew caught all of this on film.

Inside the beat-up, black Town Car, I began to regain my focus. Filth lined the floor. The humidity was so high, my shirt was drenched in sweat just from that brief period outside, and I was sticking to the seats.

Welcome back to Florida, I thought as I wondered how I'd ever lived in this sauna.

The AC felt cold, but not cold enough to take away my nausea and sweats. I didn't know if it was from anxiety or the pills, but one thing was clear in my mind: *this is as good a time as any to go to treatment, because these damn pills aren't doing anything anymore.* They just wouldn't kick in.

"How much further?" I kept asking like a kid on his way to Disney. Except I wasn't wagging my tail out of excitement. I feared I would puke everywhere.

It suddenly hit me why the Town Car was so filthy and nasty. It was used to transport those like me who emptied their guts onto the floor.

The folks overseeing the filming scooted away from me, recognizing that my green appearance might be signaling a sudden eruption.

Let's just get there, I said to myself.

The drive from Ft. Lauderdale to Lake Worth took forever. It's a good thing we weren't going all the way to Disney, because I couldn't have made it. We were in traffic, and I watched the cars whirring by, periodically slamming on their brakes for a backup before getting released again like racehorses.

Crazy Florida drivers.

All these people were going home from their jobs or to the gym or the grocery store—normal, respectable stuff—and I was trying my best not to puke on a bunch of people I barely knew. I leaned against that door, praying that my guts would stay inside of me.

Finally, after what seemed like forever, we stopped. Somebody opened my door, and I didn't even have the strength to stop myself from falling out. I put my hands onto pavement as the rest of my body slammed against the solid surface.

I'd taken a lot of hits, but nothing quite this humbling—not even having my picture with Randy White manhandling me plastered on the Hall of Fame walls.

When I fell outside that treatment center, nobody tried to help me up from that concrete. I'll never know why. I mean, it's not like you see guys falling out of cars all the time. Maybe they figured this would create more dramatic footage.

I was only about thirty feet from the entrance to a place where everyone apparently hoped I could find my life again. But I wasn't sure I would make it to the door.

I knew I had to try, so I dragged my feet out from under my body, and I started crawling. My skinny, grey body scraped behind me. I had lost so much weight; you'd never guess I'd played center. You'd never had guessed I'd played anything.

As I crawled forward towards the entrance, I left behind traces of my skin and blood. I guess it was appropriate to crawl, since I was sort of like an infant—experiencing my first true attempt at getting *recentered.*

I wouldn't have believed it at the time, but September 22, 2009, would mark the last day I ever used benzos or opiates. People ask me why treatment worked this time. I can't say there was one magic ticket—or even a single reason. I think it was a combination of factors.

Lydia thinks it's because I had all these people to be accountable to, since I was getting help with the surgeries and treatment, and I had a camera crew watching me 24-7. In other words, I had the increased pressure of public shame to force me to get it right. But if the shame of having my then fifteen-year-old daughter seeing her dad pass out and my son having to hold me down during a hallucination didn't force me to get it right, I don't know how the shame from strangers would have pushed me over the tipping point.

Whatever it was, I knew that I'd finally run out of lanes. In football, my job was to prevent the other guy from getting to my quarterback. In effect, I was cutting off that lane. The drugs I'd been pounding for years cut off my lanes to any positive emotion. Those same drugs cut off my lanes to family, jobs, having a place to sleep, and driving a car. I came to understand that those drugs also cut off my lane to God, creating a bitterness and disbelief that He could not possibly care for me or want to serve as a guide like Dad had done.

Or to borrow from another metaphor, I was drowning. Pulling myself across the concrete slab of that parking lot brought me back to being eight years old and pinned by that paddleboat under water. I felt like I couldn't breathe, and my lungs were ready to explode. Fear engulfed me as I struggled to break the surface.

But this time, I had hands reaching for me. I couldn't see them yet, but they were inside those doors, waiting to pull me from the depths into a place where I could breathe again.

They say people won't change unless the pain of changing becomes less than the pain of staying the same. I knew that I would die if I continued. I had no options left except one: *to fight for my life with the desperation of a drowning man.*

Sometimes I wonder if I would have gotten help if I'd had one last open lane. *What if my car hadn't broken down? What if my mom could have bailed me out one more time? What if I hadn't played my last card?*

But on the flip side, I also wonder, *what would have happened if I'd gotten sober sooner? What if I could have been there for my daughter's sweet sixteen, instead of wasting it away, high in bed? Or been the father to my son, like my dad was to me?* I can ask myself, but I have to let those thoughts go, because they can easily pull me back underwater.

Detox usually takes seven to ten days. But knowing how bad my seizures were, the facility kept me in detox for a month. They wanted to play it safe. Also, with the documentary crew around, they didn't want anything going haywire—which meant not a single seizure. With the film crew following me every second, I had no privacy outside of using the toilet or in therapy.

I felt absolutely miserable, physically and emotionally. All I wanted to do was isolate and sleep. So that's what I did. And when I slept, I obsessed about using. In my dreams, I was throwing down pills by the handful. It had been such a big part of my life. My knee was hurting. My neck was hurting. The meds they were giving me didn't even scratch the surface of my aches.

Two weeks into detox, I pulled myself out of bed and sat outside at a picnic table with a pen and notebook. I wasn't prepared for what happened next. Typically, I'd get up and make videos with a camera they'd given me, then I'd sit and write down my thoughts. That was my new routine. My therapist told me that writing was a great way to get things out. While that might be true, my writing only came out in small drips, so I never really *got things out.* Until that day.

As I sat writing, with my body leaning over that rough slab of wood, tears started rolling down my face like boulders being released from inside. The guilt, the shame, every selfish act I'd committed hit me suddenly and more brutally than having my legs snapped in front of me. Now sober, the emotions held back by drugs overwhelmed me, and the avalanche began. I hadn't been one to cry, so this was something that I felt God was orchestrating.

With a sense that I had His ear, I asked, *God,* will *this obsession ever lift?* I was in misery, needing pills more than ever to take away this unwanted barrage of negative emotions.

"Hey, group starts in fifteen minutes," someone said from just behind me. At that very second, it felt like somebody draped a warm quilt around my shoulders. I had the sensation of a physical, warm weight on my shoulders, comforting; not at all like the emotional boulders I'd been carrying for years.

Divine intervention. At 8:45 a.m., fifteen minutes before group therapy was to start, God reached into my heart, pulled out my heavy obsession that had always seemed too deep for me to unbury. After years of quasi-belief and faith, I experienced my spiritual awakening. God rescued me right then. That constant, cold, heavy, nagging to find more pills for just one more day disappeared instantly. Left behind was the warmth and security of that blanket, like the hug from a dear friend. My chest opened up, allowing me to breathe freely, and my burden never returned. It was as if the weight of shame, grief, and remorse was replaced by a soothing blanket. I now know it was the Holy Spirit wrapping me up—giving me complete deliverance!

I never had those feelings again about throwing down pain pills, about not liking the sensation of sobriety.

God kept showing grace to me. After detox, I became eligible to go to Mississippi for knee replacement. The doctors thought they had timed it just right, because they had me on suboxone, an opioid antagonist, to neutralize the effects of opioids. But this was God's timing, not theirs.

When they put me under for surgery, I was fine, but when I woke up and they tried to help me with my pain, nothing worked.

"Your heart's going to stop if we give you any more pain medication," they said.

Finding no relief, all I could do was lie down in the recovery room, screaming like a madman, because the pain was so brutal. There was nothing they could give me. They had just cut my bone in two places. I had to deal with it. I'd been taking pain and mood drugs for so many years, I had no pain tolerance left. It's like every hit I'd ever received in twenty-five years of football smacked me in an instant. My pain went from zero to sixty—and it kept climbing.

But I lived. I got through it. I had put others through torment for many years; in his grace, God did not allow me to suffer this intense physical pain for more than a few days.

They released me from the hospital with a full bottle of Percocet in my hand. To get back to the treatment center, I had to ride alone by a car service from Columbia, Mississippi, to Birmingham, Alabama.

So what do you think I did?

Any other time in my post NFL life, I would have taken a handful of pills from that bottle as soon as I got in the car. Not this time. *Not again*, I emphatically told myself.

When I arrived at the intake desk back at the treatment center, I handed over the pill bottle I'd been holding.

"Randy, it looks like they are all there," the woman said after counting them. I hadn't taken a single pill.

"Yes, Ma'am," I said. "They are all there."

For the first time in decades, I felt a moment of pride take over me, almost like when a coach had said, "Well played, Grimes," after a really good drill or play.

Maybe I can do this, I thought.

Once back in treatment, they sent me for another week of detox just to purge all the surgery meds out of my system. Then I entered the treatment center.

After meeting others in treatment, I became grateful that I'd never discovered heroin. With all the doctors' prescriptions and buying drugs on the streets, I'd never even heard the word heroin. It had to have been a geographical thing. Maybe in Houston, the influx hadn't happened there yet.

Lydia calls it a God thing. She's probably right.

I felt like I could breathe for the first time in years, maybe the first time ever.

In that moment also, I realized that I needed to make all my struggles and the pain I created for others to *mean something.* I needed to give back. I needed what I lost when football ended: a purpose.

CHAPTER THIRTY-THREE

THE INTERVENTION

"Take the first step in faith. You don't have to see the whole staircase, just take the first step."

—MARTIN LUTHER KING JR.

December 27, 2018

"Bobby's in detox," Travis told me over the phone. "He was in rough shape. He's doing better today. He'll probably be ready to leave in a couple of days." Detox can last a few days to a couple of weeks in more extreme cases.

"He failed the drug test," Travis continued. "He said that he didn't take anything the day he came in, but that's not what the test showed. And we found a couple of Vicodin in his coat pocket."

As I mentioned, trying to smuggle in an emergency stash of drugs is common. I took a young man and young woman into treatment a few years before. On the plane, the boy handed his girlfriend the plastic wrap from the bottom of his cigarette pack when she went to the bathroom. I didn't think much of it at the time. Turns out, they worked out a plan ahead of time. The girl had dope in her purse. Wrapping it in the plastic from his cigarette wrapper, she inserted it into her body. Fortunately, addiction specialists have been there before and know what to look for. And they know, um, where to look. Her stash didn't make it past intake.

"Hey, tell him I said hello. And let him know that I'll give him a week or two before I come see him. Will you do that?" I asked Travis.

"Let me play that by ear," Travis answered. "He's hating the world right now. Hearing your name might not be a good thing."

"I understand," I told him honestly.

I remember those *hating the world* days. They were long, and I didn't know I could cry that long without running out of tears. I just wanted the pain to stop. I couldn't tell if my body or my emotions were hurting the most. I felt like a meteor entering the Earth's atmosphere. Fire shot out from around me as I sped toward impact. Fortunately, just when I thought I couldn't take it anymore, God gave me some landing gear and helped me touch down without blowing into a million pieces.

A week later, just after the new year, I popped in to see Bobby between afternoon meetings. Travis told me that Bobby was in a better place, and that he could use some encouragement.

I remembered from my treatment that it didn't matter if you smoked or not. When you had a few minutes between meetings, almost everyone went outside to the smoking area.

I had one mission: *check in on Bobby*.

I went to the large, covered pavilion where the smokers hung out. As I got closer, I saw Bobby.

"How they treating you, buddy?" I put an arm around his shoulder.

When Bobby recognized me, his face lit up.

"Hey Randy!" he said excitedly. "I thought you abandoned me."

"You kidding?" I shot back. "You can't get rid of me that easy. You look good, man. Your color is great, and I think you've put on a pound or two. Looks good on you."

"Thanks, I feel pretty good now," Bobby said. "But I thought I was going to die when I first got here."

"Withdrawals?" I asked with empathy.

"Yeah," he nodded as he took a puff on his cigarette. "I couldn't sleep. Every time I ate, I puked. My head felt like it was going to pop."

"That's all that crap coming out of your body," I agreed. "It's part of the process. And it's not one you want to have to go through again. Just remember that," I said with a slight laugh.

"I don't even remember the first week," Bobby continued. "Honestly, I wanted to die, but I couldn't think clearly. Then they gave me some vitamins and stuff. Those helped me sleep. As I started to feel better, I could eat again. Now that's all I want to do," he said. "Well, sleep, eat, and smoke," he added.

"One day at a time, brother. And one thing at a time, too," I encouraged him. "So what are you learning? Do you have time to give me a little rundown?"

By this time, most of the others in the pavilion had started to head back inside. Breaks were short by design.

"Shoot," I said as I looked around. "Looks like I came in between meetings. Let me walk you back," I offered.

"My mom and sister are coming next weekend to visit me," Bobby said with a smile. "I've talked to my mom a couple of times. She called in for a counseling session," Bobby said. "And I've talked to Julia and Anna, too. They are going to try to come the next weekend," he said, his face breaking into a broad smile. "I've missed them so much. I don't know what happened to me. I started thinking of Julia as my enemy. But God, I miss her."

We stood outside Bobby's meeting room and continued talking, until the meeting leader came to shut the door, signaling the meeting was beginning.

"It's great to see you looking healthy, Bobby!" I told him honestly. "Lydia wanted me to tell you that she's still praying, every single morning."

"Thank you, Randy," he said, initiating a hug. "Thank you for everything. Come again soon, okay?" he asked.

After I watched him walk through the door, I leaned up against the wall.

"Lord, thank You for watching over Bobby and getting him this far. Please continue to give him strength to do the hard things, the things You want him to do so he can live his fullest life. Amen."

I stayed in touch with Bobby, stopping by every couple of days to encourage him and see if he needed anything.

I feel like I adopt those I help get into treatment. While I can't stay with them 24/7 as they do their own hard work of recovery, I feel a sense of responsibility for them.

As the weekend of Julia's and Anna's visit approached, Lydia had an idea. "After they have their family session on Saturday morning, why don't you and Bobby spend time with Anna while I take Julia out to talk?" she offered.

My addiction involved descending into the abyss, creating a maelstrom that sucked every good thing in behind me. Although I enjoy working with families, I feel more skilled at working with the person who is the source of pain.

Lydia's experience was different from mine. She suffered as a wife, partner, friend, and parent. She did everything to reach me, to get me help. But in the end, she was as powerless as I was over my addiction. As much as I felt a calling to take hope to those struggling to overcome alcohol and drugs, Lydia heard the calling to minister to family members, especially wives whose husbands had disappeared into a bottle, needle, or pill.

"I like it," I told her. "Maybe I can take them out fishing around Singer Island."

"It's too cold to be on the water," Lydia cautioned.

"It is for us, but not for them," I reminded her. "It will be 75 degrees today. It was snowing in Georgia."

January 23, 2017

Lydia and I arrived at the treatment center just as the family finished their second session with Travis. As Bobby, Julia, and Anna walked outside into the sunlight, it dawned on me that I had never seen them together before, as a family. My heart warmed when I saw that Anna walked between her parents, her little hands holding theirs on either side. We waved and shouted greetings to each other. After we all hugged, I leaned down to greet Anna.

"Hi, I'm Randy...So how old are you?" I said as I straightened up and pretended to study her more carefully. "I'm guessing you're probably eighteen, maybe nineteen years old..."

"Noooooo!" Anna said in a high-pitched, sweet voice. "Six!"

"That was my second guess," I said with a wink. "Well, Anna, I am so glad to finally meet you. Are you ready to go to the beach this morning?"

"Yes!" she affirmed as she jumped up and down. "I want to go swimming!"

"Well, we'll see about swimming when we get there," I laughed. "It might be a bit cold."

Lydia and Julia peeled off a few minutes later, and Bobby, Anna, and I headed in my truck to the beach. Once we were there and Anna was distracted carving designs with shells in the sand, I had a moment with Bobby.

"You look better every time I see you, man," I said honestly. "Do you feel different? How are the cravings? Are you still struggling with urges to..., you know?" I asked.

"I don't have cravings to get high," Bobby said. "I've been seeing the chiropractor, and he's really loosened up my shoulder. It doesn't hurt like it used to...but I'm still struggling. Our first session this morning was rough," he admitted. "I want to talk reconciliation, but Julia is still not ready. And as soon as I felt shut down, my hands started to shake. Like, out of nowhere, after, after a great week, I wanted my pills."

"Your emotions mess with you, right?" I asked. "I thought I had a physical pain problem that made me abuse drugs. But I found out pretty quick in recovery that I had both physical and emotional pain to deal with."

"Yeah," Bobby nodded. "Travis said that I have a fear of abandonment. When I feel like I'm being left, I do the leaving by pouring something down my throat and popping pills. Travis saw that I was upset this morning, and he called me out on it."

"What did he say?"

"He said, 'What just happened? Your face changed when Julia said she's not ready to talk about you coming back home.' And I didn't want to answer him. I wanted to yell, storm out of the room, and find a bar. But he kept asking, 'What are you thinking?' So finally, I told him. And then he says, 'That's great. We're getting somewhere. You felt those bad things, you talked about it, but you didn't drink,'" Bobby shared.

"Whew," I said with a whistle, "That's a breakthrough, buddy. You're ahead of where I was when I went to treatment," I told him sincerely. "It took me a while to learn that I could talk about things without my emotions taking me to buy drugs."

The three of us spent a little time at Singer Island, and then I brought them up to my place. As soon as we got inside, Anna ran to the sliding door by the balcony and asked to go out.

"Sure," I told her as I pulled the doors open. "Hey, let me show you something. If you look right down here," I pointed to the water down below, "You might get lucky and see a stingray or a manatee."

"What's a manatee?" she asked. "Manatees are sometimes called sea cows," I answered. "They are huge sea mammals, and just like cows, they eat plants. And they can get as big as a car," I told her.

"Whoaaaaaa!" Anna squealed. "I want to see one!"

"Keep your eyes open, and you just might," I suggested.

Bobby didn't make it as far as the balcony. Instead, he stopped in the living room, looking at a few game balls and trophies in my display cabinet.

"So you really were a football player," Bobby said, eyeing the collection.

"Did you think I was lying?" I teased.

"No, but seeing them here," he trailed off. "Wow. That's something. Do you miss it? Or, I guess, that's a stupid question."

"It's a good question," I told him. "For years, football was all I knew, since I was a kid. Just like you have your emotional pain that you're dealing with, I had to deal with losing something I really loved. Without football, I didn't know who I was."

"Why didn't you get into broadcasting, like working in a booth during games?" he asked.

"Well, I would have loved that job," I confided. "It wasn't in the cards for me. People knew me in Tampa Bay, but I wasn't a household name like many of the commentators are these days. I think the reason I stayed addicted for so long is that I couldn't come to terms with losing my football identity. I didn't know how to be Randy Grimes without the word football attached to my name. It was like I died, and no one even threw me a funeral."

Bobby nodded.

"For me, football was about being part of a team and sharing a goal. It meant having a playbook, working hard every day, listening to coaches, learning from those who were better than me, and doing my best," I summarized. "I didn't know that I could do that without football. But you know, I have all those things every day of my life."

"I love Julia and Anna," Bobby told me. "I don't know who I am without them. I haven't been there for them. I hope I have a chance to be part of their team again."

"Being a husband and a father is just part of who you are," I encouraged him. "But don't confuse a part for the whole. Look, I couldn't control how long my football career lasted. That was up to the coaches and owners. I could just do my part to stay in shape. But in the end, I didn't get to call the shots. So what I'm saying is, you don't get to decide what happens with you and Julia. But you do get to decide to stay on the team of recovery and be the best you can. Stick with the playbook. You're in treatment, listening to Travis, learning from people who have been where you are, and moving forward."

"I see one! I see one!" Anna shouted from the balcony.

Anna pointed down at a slow-moving mass in the water below, while jumping up and down.

"Is that a manatee?" she asked excitedly.

"It sure is!" I told her with a laugh. "And do you know something? You must be good luck. Because I've had people up here several times, and even though they keep looking, they never see one. You're like a good luck manatee spotter!" I told her.

Bobby lifted his daughter's face over the rail of the balcony so she could get a better look. The two of them giggled as the gentle giant lumbered out of sight.

Watching the pure joy in Anna's face, I remembered a similar expression that Emily had when she was that age, and a tear formed briefly, before I shifted back to Bobby.

As we headed back to meet Julia and Lydia, I shared one more thing with Bobby.

"That look on Anna's face when she saw the manatee?" I asked. "Did you see it?"

"Yeah," Bobby said. "That made my day. Probably my whole week."

"She reminded me of my children, Emily and Brady, when they were that age," I confided. "But during that time, I was Randy Grimes, football player and budding drug addict. I saw joy on her face, along with sadness at times. And even though I was with her, I wasn't present, sharing the world with her. I was lost in myself. You have such a great gift getting clean and sober now, so you can really be there for your girl."

"Thank you for reminding me of that," Bobby said. "Thank you for being such a good friend." After a short pause, he added, "And coach to me."

And that may have made my entire day.

CHAPTER THIRTY-FOUR

RANDY'S STORY

"God sends the dawn that we might see the might-have-beens that still might be."

—Robert Brault

After my recovery, my definition of *self* changed. I would no longer define myself as *Randy Grimes, Football Player*, or *Former Football Player*. And I would no longer live like *Randy Grimes: Drug Addict*. I wasn't sure yet what purpose God had for me, but I determined to find it and live it.

I had a great therapist who didn't take any of my bullshit. She helped me further work through the guilt and lost identity, replacing it with hope and a plan.

I called Lydia, and I told her that I was starting to do better. She participated in sessions with me over the phone. But none of my family came on family day. They could not afford the flights, meals, and hotel.

I think they were also waiting to see if this was real. They didn't know what to think of me anymore.

Just as I became more available to Lydia, she remained in

survival mode, feeling like she'd been thrown in a pit. Lydia attended Celebrate Recovery, and she started to understand the importance of keeping boundaries. Unfortunately for her, she didn't keep boundaries in my addiction. She was not healing. She was a classic, codependent enabler. In hindsight, she wishes she had attended Al-Anon close to her home to get the support she needed. But for the time, she stayed in a pit, miles away from me.

Most of my family was done with me, because I'd exhausted them. But they did send letters to be read in a process group of five to eight people, after I'd been there for around forty-five days. Those letters stirred me up. The people who read them acted like they were my wife, son, daughter.

From Brady

Dad,

First let me say that I love you. You had always been the figure I look to the most when I was learning what it meant to be a man, and through all of this, there was never a time when I thought you didn't love me back. Your addiction has crippled this family. Countless times I came home to your blank stare at the TV. It was not 'til later that I realized you were losing the time that we had to build our relationship. Though I knew you loved me, it was as if you were emotionally void through some of the most crucial periods of my life's development. You made a choice to be high instead of a functional father. That day in detox when you forgot your son's face was the day I started not to see the father I grew up with. Your wife loves you, never forget that. She has been through so much pain, and I have seen her broken down by a husband who has lost track of his priorities. It is sick, but sometimes it seems as though I have learned how not to live by your example. This is the end of the plank you have laid for yourself. It is time for you to stop cowering behind your escapes and face your demons head-on, because with faith in yourself and in God you are unstoppable. With this new chance to live free of burden, I am elated to have this opportunity to see you as I have always perceived you, the strongest man in the world. I miss you very much and think of you often. I love you.

Bubba

From Emily

Dad,

As usual, I am not going to be as easy on you as Mom and Brady. I am hard on you because you have not been the man you are supposed to be, who God made you to be. You were put on this earth to be a strong and mighty man, and you have not been that. You are lucky that we all even still communicate with you. You are especially lucky that you have a wife that stayed with you through the crazy things you have put her through. Every other woman in the world would have left you a long, long time ago. This past month that I haven't talked to you has been the longest we have ever gone without communication. It's sad that it had to come to this.

Why are none of us in Florida for family week? Why are these letters turned in so late? Because we are all SICK of it. Sick of rehabs, sick of drugs, sick of you not just being normal, sick and tired of your addiction STILL being a part of our lives. It won't go away!! For the love of God, just stop!! If you want to bad enough, you will get clean. You haven't wanted to get clean bad enough.

The last thing you told me on the phone a month ago was, "If you have issues with me, you have money, get therapy." First of all, no one should say that to their daughter. And secondly, let's talk about WHY I have issues with you. Let's start from the brutal beginning. In 1992, I was eight years old playing on the beach and I witnessed you having a seizure for the first time. I still will never forget that moment. I thought you were dying. Come to find out, you were getting off Halcion and seized. This was the beginning of your being selfish with drugs instead of thinking about what it was doing to your family that had to witness it. To make it worse, Brady was only four. ... [Years later,] You almost died getting off something, and the paramedics shocked you back to life. You seemed to be a bit better for a few years, but in 2005 it came out you were very addicted to Xanax. In '05 and '06 you listened to me and Mom planning my wedding and stressing and worrying about how we were going to pay for it, and you had a secret account!! It still blows my mind! Since '05, it has been bad. When we were still at the Kingscourt house, I watched you stare at the TV in a stupor all day. Your eyes would be almost closed, your Copenhagen would be all over your face and dripping down your shirt, and your speech was always so slurred that it was heartbreaking. I tried many, many, many times to talk to you and beg you to stop. I told you that because I love you so much, I just want you well. Brady and I were not comfortable ever having friends over because you were so messed up and slurring and saying weird things. On my wedding day, you were out of Xanax, and were probably about to have a seizure, so Mom had to give you money for Xanax so you could make it through my wedding and walk your only daughter down the aisle. Then in '07 Hudson was born. He loves you and still talks about you every day. I am sad for him because he doesn't have a normal grandpa. He deserves a grandpa that will be clean and sober and will take him to do things, take him fishing. I can't even let him in the car with you. Think about all the times you had a seizure shortly after me and Hudson were in the car with you. It's just not worth it. And now I have another one on the way. If for any reason, get clean for your grandbabies. Over the years I have probably seen 15–20 seizures, called many ambulances, and had major anxiety because of you. In '06, I was home alone, I heard the motor running very loud in the driveway and ran outside to find you seizing, choking on your tongue, and pushing the gas pedal down with your foot while the car was in park. I was totally freaking out. I called 911 as usual, but after that incident I became extremely anxious and thought I was having heart problems. It was anxiety attacks, and yes, I blame that on you. No one should have to see their dad like that over and over and over.

As far as Mom, in '82 you said wedding vows that you would take care of her and provide for her. Well, she is homeless right now, so you aren't doing a very good job. You have broken all your wedding vows. She has supported you, herself, and Brady in college for almost three years on a teacher's salary...not easy. You have chosen the drugs over her, and I know you always say you haven't. But you have. The drugs are the only reason you and Mom have problems. And it makes me furious when you talk about her being too close to her parents. How dare you!? The extremes you have put us through and the severity of your addiction are not even comparable to her minor faults. So don't go there. Don't talk bad about the one person who has stood by your side 'til the bitter end and defended you to countless people. She has had to rely on her parents financially and emotionally, because she hasn't had a husband. You have not been there for her emotionally, financially, physically, anything. You should thank God every second she is still married to you and that you still have a chance to work this out. You and I both know that she is the most beautiful woman inside and out, and you know there are men out there that would worship her, take care of her, and be a good husband to her. If you don't want that to happen, you better act quick.

You always say, "Worry about your own family," and I really do. I am busy with my husband and son, and I really don't live in the past. Obviously, your addiction has had a big effect on me and was a distinct part of my life. But I know God is healing me, and I am strong. I am going to be okay. However, I hate what you have done to Brady. You yourself were so affected by your own father and you loved him so much, that it's hard to believe what you have done to your own kids. You blame your dad's death with a lot of your emotional pain. Ironically, you took drugs to numb the pain, and in turn became a bad father yourself. Brady has been dealing with your addiction his whole life. There were only a few years in there where you were normal. He has seen, heard, dealt with way too much for a twenty-one-year-old. He is a college junior, and he knows you haven't put one dime into his schooling. He sees dads coming up to the campus and going to games with their sons; he needs a dad. He hasn't had a father figure, and I worry about what that will do to him in the future. He has seen about the same number of seizures that I have. When you were hallucinating last year in the psych ward at the hospital, he went up there, and you didn't even know him and were trying to fight him. That's when he drew the line in the sand; he was done with you. You have been a horrible example of what a father and husband should be. I know there were good times in there, but the bad times were so bad that they take over the good. Thankfully, Brady is an amazing person and very involved in his hobbies and school.

The crazy part is I still love you so much. All I want is for you to be normal. I would like for you and Mom to work it out and fall back in love and you be the husband she deserves. I would like for you to be able to be clean and healthy. I would like to have family barbecues, vacations, things normal families do. The future is in your hands. You choose the path.

If you remember anything from this letter, it is that I just want you to be broken, truly broken. Broken before God, letting all your pride down, and saying "God, without You, I am nothing. Forgive me. Save me." I want you to come to the end of yourself and your filthy past and be done with it.

"Amazing grace, how sweet the sound, that saved a wretch like me. I once was lost but now I'm found, was blind but now I see."

I love you.

Emy

From Lydia

I want to start by saying how grateful I am for the surgery and help with drug detox and therapy. This has been a miracle from the Lord that your knee has been repaired and the need for painkillers will soon be gone. I can't say thank you enough for this gift we've been given. I'm proud that you have stayed at [the center] and are learning how to deal with your own addictions. I truly regret I didn't make it to your surgery. I shouldn't have let the timing and travel make my decision. I know I should have been there, and I'm so sorry. I didn't have the money for the plane ticket to get to family week, and Emily's pregnancy is so fragile right now. I know you understand. I would have liked to have been there for my own healing too.

Remembering back... I fell crazy in love with you the first day of Baylor thirty years ago. You were a big 'ol East Texas boy in your Wranglers with a sweet smile, and big brown cow eyes. I remember how much we talked and how you made me laugh. Three years later, we were married before our senior year. We lived in half a duplex. Life was so simple then. We were happy as could be with no money, just love. We left for Tampa a year later, blessed with your job and pregnant with Emily. Then a few years later, we had another blessing: Brady. During this time in football, I knew you took pills to sleep, but never realized the addiction until you had a seizure from Halcion withdrawal in 1991. You stayed on sleep medicine for years, but I never saw it affect you during the day. We spent four years after football living off the money and trying to figure out what we were going to do with our lives. You went to work with a concrete company. By 1999, I was seeing you slurred, sleeping more, and increasingly agitated. Then you began taking cocaine and drinking. During that next year, Emily found you passed out on the floor. You drove your truck into the water on Emily's sixteenth birthday and couldn't remember where the truck was. You nearly died from an overdose on our moving day. You quit cocaine and seemed to be trying to stay clean. You've always been so good at hiding everything. The next few years were very, very hard, and we were so busy with the children in high school and college. You had gotten a great job at Acme Brick and were working your way up. The drugs seemed to be a night thing again.

But by 2005, money was missing even though you had a great job. You admitted how addicted you were to Xanax. I again thought I could help and tried to change you. I went to doctors with you and enabled you. I know encouragement and help turned into enabling. I knew the pain in your neck and knee was increasing. You have been in and out of six rehabs and never stuck with any of them. I tried to understand the addiction, but I couldn't. Problems at work started showing up when they took your accounts away in 2006. We were hurting financially trying to make it on my teaching salary. By June 2007, you were fired when you were messed up in front of the president of the company. I have been supporting us ever since.

Your choices have devastated our family and marriage. This has taken you to depths so low I could never have imagined you would do the things you've done. You had 10 percent of your salary going into a secret account just for drug money. You took my jewelry and pawned it. You bought back the ring your dad gave me, only to pawn it again. You sold your Southwest Conference ring and the NFL ring for drug money. You took sentimental antique fans and clocks your dad had restored and gave us and sold them. You bought drugs off the street from sleazy drug dealers and put your own family in danger. You only think of yourself and your needs, not what this has done to your children. They have needed a father—someone to look up to. You have not even helped pay for any of Brady's college, and he's a junior. I did use your retirement paycheck last month to help.

We have watched you have countless seizures, called ambulances, and witnessed crazy hallucinations. This has had horrible lasting effects and been traumatic for our children, more than you even realize or want to understand. The kids have been humiliated by you. Their friends have seen you sitting in your La-Z-Boy, head hanging down, eyes drooping and speech slurred, way too many times. I have pleaded and begged you to change.

Because of all the lies, rejection, and betrayal, our marriage has deteriorated. I have been so alone physically and mentally.

In the middle of all this, God has wrapped His arms around me and given me a peace and rest only He can give.

I have worked, our children have graduated from high school and gone to college. We've had a wedding and a grandson born. I just keep trying to keep it all together. I'm paying all the bills and trying to pay the debts. We are now homeless. You are living off your $900 from the NFL, and I'm living with my parents. You have taken money from your mother, sister, brother, and my parents. It's not right!!

I am forty-eight years old, and all I ever wanted was to grow old with you, and we could take care of each other. I can't even remember what it's like to be happy as a couple. We have been so blessed with our children and family. You have cheated us all of a husband, father, and grandfather.

I didn't know if I should write this, or if you would even hear my words. It's always about you. You have become a manipulator and a con artist.

I have stayed married to you, because I have held on, waiting for God to heal you. I know this will happen only if you want to be healed. I also made a covenant to you on our wedding day and have remained faithful. Many people have said I should leave and move on with my life. I just haven't been able to.

Where do we go from here? I want to see change and repentance. Even the prodigal son came to himself, and his actions showed it. I believe in new beginnings; when will it start? I haven't changed my beliefs or morals since the first day you met me. You are the one who walked out of my life. What has changed is that I am sad and lonely. I miss being married, and I want you to be the man that God wants you to be. I don't want to be this angry, frustrated, and disappointed person that I've become. I know I have unforgiveness that I need to deal with. I feel like I've been thrown in a pit without doing anything to deserve it. God is showing me that I can forgive, and it doesn't make what has happened right, but it will make me better. God has allowed all of this to happen to us, and I can only be open to how he wants to use me through this and use you to help others.

I talk to you on the phone and hope I hear something in your voice that shows me how broken you are. Your family needs you to be healed and take responsibility. Be the husband, father, and grandfather, son, and brother to the ones who have loved you unconditionally.

I give God praise for giving me the strength I need. The joy of the Lord is my strength.

I will always love you.

"For I know the plans I have for you, declares the Lord, plans to prosper you and not to harm you, plans to give you hope and a future." —Jeremiah 29:11

"I waited patiently for the Lord, and he inclined to me and heard my cry. He also brought me up out of a horrible pit, out of the miry cay and set my feet upon a rock, and established my steps. He has put a new song in my mouth praise to our God, many will see it and fear, And will put their trust in the Lord." —Psalm 40

Lydia

I sobbed at the reading of the letters. Hearing their words reinforced why I was there. Just as God had been working in my heart, he began changing Lydia. She started offering me her forgiveness, and her bitterness started to slip away. Not overnight. I hadn't become a raging drug addict immediately. It took years to slip into that state. And I knew the healing of Lydia's broken heart wouldn't mend instantly, either.

I was in treatment for ninety days total, sixty of which were intensive therapy.

I got out three days before Christmas and flew back to Texas. Lydia hardly recognized me. I was full of life. I was tan and fit. I'd been chauffeured to the gym and cooked for by a chef every day.

I wanted her to be happy to see me, and I think she was. But I also think she was asking herself: *How does that happen? You're the one who put us through hell while I held things together, but YOU are getting the special treatment?*

The aftercare plan was to go right back to the halfway house after Christmas. Momma got me a truck and a phone, and back to Florida I went.

It wasn't easy leaving Lydia again. I think she thought I'd be gone a month.

But I was desperate to do whatever the treatment professionals told me to, so I moved into sober living with a bunch of kids in Del Ray. I was forty-nine. I was willing to do it, because I didn't really want to be discharged. I'd gone through treatment, but I still had so much to learn. I needed to be in that community of recovery, as much as I'd needed to be around my team when learning how to be a pro player. I needed to watch how others did it, so I could try it myself, until those plays became routine.

I still needed that "locker room" community that I'd lost. I needed other guys keeping me accountable and relating their struggles and triumphs.

Sober living lasts as long as you want it to. My roommate and I lived in a house with six other guys. We had meetings two to three times a day. I went to the treatment facility often, doing anything I could to stick around. I'd hang out with my people around the smoking circle. And when they returned to their meetings, I walked the grounds, searching for cigarette butts to pick up. I did it as part of giving back, and it gave back to me by helping me retain my sobriety. At the end of some days, my fingers smelled so bad that soap couldn't remove the stench.

"You're not coming home yet?" Lydia asked after I hadn't come home for months. She was still paying off our debt, while I seemed to be becoming a Floridian.

In March, I met Lydia on her spring break in Melbourne, Florida, where she'd come to see our daughter and son-in-law who was in spring training for baseball. I told her I was afraid to return to Houston. I knew if I went back, I would fall right back into the groove of destruction I'd carved so deep. I played the tape all the way through. I knew every time I got out of treatment in Houston, I went back to using. I knew in the same environment so early in my recovery, I'd return to the same old Randy. *I couldn't trust myself.*

"So I got a job working with alumni," I told her.

"You what?" she asked, smiling at me, while her eyes showed sadness. She didn't see this as part of the deal when I went off for treatment—that I would not come back.

"I love you," I responded, wishing that could take away her pain, while knowing that it wasn't enough.

She knew I wouldn't change my mind, so she resigned herself to living states apart, paying off my debt while she lived with her parents. All the stuff from our house was still in storage. She couldn't get her own place, because she didn't have the money.

Besides, Texas was her home. I don't think she could understand why I couldn't survive there—let alone be happy.

From sober living, I moved into a single-bedroom place that would be my own. I stayed for another three months. I finally moved toward West Palm Beach by the airport into a one-bedroom bungalow.

Florida was a new start, a chance to push the reset button. I hadn't screwed anybody over in Florida, hadn't pawned anything in Florida, hadn't gotten high in Florida. Everything was good in Florida, and it was easier for me to keep it that way.

We lived parallel lives for seven years. I called her every day. I gave her no clarity, other than me living in another state, building my career, and deepening my recovery.

Two of my grandbabies were born, and while I flew back for holidays, I wasn't there to know them day-to-day like Lydia was. She stayed busy with her own work and the grandchildren, and I'm sure most people encouraged her to get over me.

As I could afford it, even outside of holidays, I would fly out to see Lydia, or she would fly out to see me. Lydia spent most of the summer with me, and when we were apart, we spoke on the phone several times a day. I asked her to move to Florida to be with me, but she was teaching and helping with grandbabies. She wanted me to move to Texas, but I knew I couldn't do that. At least not yet.

For some reason—I guess it was that God-induced faith in our potential future restoration—she didn't stop talking to me or visiting me.

"I prayed and prayed, asking God what I should do," Lydia later told me. "And I got a peace when I felt Him say, 'I love Randy. I want to heal him. I want to restore your family.' I didn't stick around because I was too worn out to leave you or because I'm a good person. I'm here because God promised me restoration." She never gave up hope in the promise God had made to restore me. And I'm forever grateful.

Lydia also says she never stopped praying for me.

And I never stopped loving Lydia with my whole heart—or thinking that she was the most stunning creature on the planet. I never stopped believing she was the kindest woman that walked this Earth.

To me, it all made sense. I was taking care of myself first, because I could never take care of her if I didn't. And when I was whole enough, I wanted nothing more than to have her by my side. My intention was not to reject or abandon Lydia—or end our marriage. But showing her that I was trustworthy would take us a long time.

Bringing two lives together after so many years apart would mean that the marriage we restarted would be a different one than we'd known before. She would have to get to know the sober me. And I would have to be the man she deserved.

In 2016, Lydia finally took the step to move to Florida with me. That took our healing to a new level, and we thank God for the miracle of His mercy and grace.

CHAPTER THIRTY-FIVE

THE INTERVENTION

*"The roots of all goodness lie in the soil of
appreciation for goodness."*

—DALAI LAMA

January 24, 2019

Lydia and I saw Bobby a few more times before he finished the program. When it came time for his graduation ceremony, we were there along with Wilma. "He looks better than I've seen him for years," Wilma gushed. "He looks like his old self again."

"Sobriety looks great on him," I agreed. "He's probably put on twenty-five pounds of muscle. I'm glad I don't have to block him in football!"

Few occasions make me as excited as seeing someone successfully complete a treatment program. It's the same sense of awe I get when I watch the Paralympics. Instead of quitting or not even starting to compete, these athletes dismiss every excuse and fight their way to the top. When it comes to recovering addicts, they may not have lost use of their limbs, but they've lost their foundations. Addiction removes their best parts. I lost my values. All that remained was a shell. Recovery gives us a second chance to compete and fight our way to a better life.

When it came time for Bobby to stand up to say a few words to those assembled at the ceremony, he walked with confidence.

"I have so many people to thank for being here today. Like my sweet mom," he said, pointing her out and waving.

Several folks in the room clapped.

"My mom never lost faith in me, even when I gave up on myself. She wanted so badly for me to get help that she called this hulking giant to come grab me out of bed. He held me by the throat and threatened me with grave bodily harm if I didn't come down here," Bobby told the room as he pointed to me. "Seriously, that's Randy Grimes, and he's become a hero. Randy and his wife, Lydia, came out to Georgia to help me.

"I can say this now, but when I agreed to go to treatment, I planned on going through the motions. I didn't have a lot of options left. I figured I'd take this little vacation," Bobby said as everyone in the room laughed.

"And you graduating with me know this is a vacation you never want to have again!" Again, everyone laughed.

"I had a little bottle of pills with me, and I figured they would keep me sane until I learned where to get some more down here. I mean, how hard could it be to find drugs in a treatment center full of drug addicts?" he laughed.

"But something happened to me along the way," Bobby said, turning serious. "I realized that God had given me so much to be thankful for, things I forgot about when I started using. By the time I got through detox, I knew one thing for sure: *never again*. But I still wasn't happy. I may have been sober, but I wasn't living yet. Along the way, the stuff I heard in those meeting rooms, the things some of you shared with me, and the ideas that Travis opened my eyes to see.... Well, at some point I forgot to be miserable. After about three weeks here, I was ready to admit that I was powerless over alcohol, and my life had become unmanageable."

Several people in the audience clapped loudly, and a few said, "Hi, Bobby!" and "Welcome, Bobby!"

If you're not a recovering alcoholic or substance abuser, the laughing and cheering at what seemed to be inappropriate times would disturb you. Before I entered recovery, I pictured twelve-step meetings filled with chain-smoking, ninety-year-old men who cussed and raged against how much they missed drinking! But that's not the case. Joy filled this space. People celebrated because they, too, had once been lost but were found. This room was full of those who had been struggling with an addiction or experiencing pain from loving someone who struggled with an addiction. Many of those graduating would claim each other as brothers and sisters, some of them remaining closer than blood relatives, even years later. Where they had shared the bondages of addiction, they were set free.

"I've just started putting it all together. I have miles to go. I've started making my amends, but it'll be a long process," he continued.

"I want to thank Travis and the other awesome counselors I've worked with here." He pointed and waved to Travis. "Randy told me to learn the playbook, and I've started that. Then he told me to surround myself with the right people, who I could learn from. Travis, that's what you've done for me, and even though I'm going back home, you know I'll still be calling you every day for a few years, right?"

Travis laughed and nodded, "Of course!"

"I was told to keep it under an hour," Bobby laughed, like he was enjoying his role as speaker. "So let me end with two more things. First, could we all say a silent prayer for those who are still suffering with addiction?" Bobby lowered his head and closed his eyes.

As I said a silent prayer, I remembered the faces of fellow athletes who, like me, started down the path to addiction during their playing days, but never stopped until they died from overdoses. I thought of my buddy, whose tragic and early death had spurred me to recover my life. I saw the faces of Lydia, Emily, and Brady who begged me to get help, but I was not ready to surrender. Then I recalled the countless, repeated headlines of another son, daughter, brother, sister, mother, father, friend, or neighbor dead because the lies of addiction told them it was *too late to get out alive*. Finally, I asked God to show me those who needed help, so I could be an instrument of His peace, forgiveness, and healing.

After a few moments, Bobby pointed at the ceiling and folded his hands in front of his chest.

"My last thank you is to You, my heavenly Father, for never leaving me, never forsaking me, and helping me find my way back to You."

Everyone in the room stood up and applauded as Bobby closed, several yelling, "Amen," in the process.

"Amen," I leaned over and said quietly into Lydia's ear.

"Amen," Lydia whispered back as she hugged me to her.

CHAPTER THIRTY-SIX

RANDY'S STORY

*"Thank God for his grace, for without it
we would have no hope!"*

—BILLY GRAHAM

When I was driving that broken-down Range Rover all over Houston looking for pills, with a heap of clothes in the back and no one who trusted me, who would have thought that one day, I'd be of use? And who could have dreamed that my use would involve helping others get out of their addiction?

Who would have thought that *my story* could help someone else?

You could say that helping others into recovery was all I had. But truth is, recovery was all I needed. Because in *recovery* —which literally meant repossessing the parts that had been covered or lost—I regained my life, my family, and my relationship with God.

When I received this gift of recovery—and I mean truly received, to where it was a part of me—I knew I needed to help others who were still struggling. That's all I wanted to do.

Helping others became natural, and it made football seem a lifetime ago and much less meaningful.

After a year of sobriety, I was made a full-time employee by the treatment center that had helped me get clean and find recovery.

I started by sharing my story, and then I studied how to do interventions to help shortcut the long, winding road I took to reach desperation. I worked with a mentor in New Jersey. Parents brought their loved ones to see this man in his office. He would do one intervention right after another, then ship them off to treatment. I would sit in and take part. I did that for over a year, witnessing hundreds of interventions. Then I started doing them with his help. Finally, I could fly solo.

Eventually, Lydia joined me in intervention work. At first, it was just because she happened to be in town, but she ended up being such a value in the process.

During the first intervention Lydia and I did together, Lydia cried with the mother, feeling the broken heart this woman had for her son. Working with families has not just helped me to heal, but I think it's helped Lydia too. It validates her suffering and gives her an outlet to use her pain to heal others. She can speak to people and provide comfort and strength they need. And sometimes she can reach someone I can't—especially family members trying to help a person with addiction. Because as you know, the addiction doesn't just affect the addict. It affects the whole family. And I like to say, *addicts get better when families get better.*

No one is immune. I've worked with guys from the NFL and MLB—as well as those who play hockey, basketball, or race-horses. I've worked with big-name athletes you've heard about and ones that aren't household names; but all, like me, are plagued by chronic pain, the adrenaline of "the game," and fear of failure.

I've also worked with celebrities, executives, CEOs—names

you know and names you don't. I've worked with rich house-wives who can't stop drinking and taking Xanax.

I work well with the "high ego" types who may have had it all—but lost it or struggled to keep it because of an addiction. I can say that with an ounce of humility, since I too wrestled with an ego bigger than myself. When guys like me can control the play of a game, or what happens on screen, or even what happens within a company, it's easy to let it go to our head. And when that control starts to wane, it's easy to turn to drugs to patch that insecurity.

But the patch wears thin, falls off, and reveals a gaping wound that only recovery—which for me, includes my Higher Power, Jesus Christ—can heal. It doesn't matter who you are or what you do, that wound resembles the next person's. We all hurt, and we all need someone to let us know we aren't alone.

I've worked with hundreds of everyday Americans like Bobby, struggling with substance abuse as a family tries to pivot around them, even as they spiral into demise.

I've also worked closely with the NFL Player Care Foundation, Baseball Assistance Team, and Sally Greer, former tennis pro, who also struggled with addiction and is now a therapist. Eric Hipple, former quarterback for the Detroit Lions, is also my colleague and friend. Eric battled depression and jumped out of a moving vehicle. He survived, but later his son died by suicide. His platform for reaching people is powerful.

I started a nonprofit, Pro Athletes in Recovery, to help guys like me.

I've been blessed to work alongside Mike Ditka and his foundation, Gridiron Greats, the same phenomenal organization that helped me when I so desperately needed it. In fact, in September of 2019, I was honored as a recipient of Mike Ditka's Gridiron Greats Hall of Fame for my recovery work with former players. My daughter, Emily, spoke on stage—fully supporting me. I was also honored with the Baylor Legends Award. My grandson, Hudson, joined me on the field to accept the award. This is the same grandson I was once not allowed to see, for fear of what I might do if I were using.

My family, true to Lydia's prayer, has been *restored*. And so has my life.

Recovery has become my playbook. *I follow it every day.*

My colleagues are my team. *I would do anything for them.*

And those with addiction are now my community. *I aim to inspire and guide them into treatment and recovery—a gift I found just in time.*

All my life, I've looked up to the greatest coach I ever had: *my dad.* When I lost him, I didn't know how to go on. Today, I aim to provide an inkling of the support he did. With God as my Father, I have found a new strength and deeper purpose. I believe anyone struggling with addiction can fill the hole in their heart, as I have with Jesus, and experience true freedom. Recovery is possible; never lose hope!

If I can help, reach out. If you know someone who needs recovery, reach out. If it's you, reach out.

Before I sign off, I'd like you to remember that I lost nearly everything in addiction, except what mattered most to me. God promised Lydia that He wanted to heal me. He did. He promised that He wanted to restore my family. He did. Today, I am closer to Emily and Garrett, and Brady and Marisa than I've ever been in my life, and I have a relationship with my grandkids that is nothing short of pure joy—and a new grandchild, Atlas, born this year.

For Lydia's part, she stayed by my side when any other woman would have left me years before. God restored our marriage.

After I'd been in recovery for a few years, my wife worked with the NFL Alumni Association and replaced the ten-year ring I sold to buy drugs. And as much as I cherish that ring, its brilliance pales against my current reality: waking up sober each day with the beautiful, forever bride—who never stopped loving me and believing that recovery could restore us.

ACKNOWLEDGMENTS

I learned early in my football days that success is a team effort. While I've had the idea to write this book for years, I needed the right team to carry it into the end zone.

I dedicate this book to my lovely wife, Lydia Brady Grimes. She is the real hero in my book. Since I met her, she's been my best friend, my prayer warrior, and the love of my life. If I were her, I'd have pushed me off a cliff years ago. In spite of everything I put Lydia through, she never stopped loving me, praying for me, and believing I could be restored to sanity.

To my children, Emily Mock and Brady Grimes, Daddy loves you very much. I gave you many reasons to lose respect for me. Thank you for letting me back into your hearts and lives. Robert Frost wrote, "*the life I live now's* an *extra life*"; I aim to spend my extra life being the daddy you always deserved.

To my son-in-law, Garrett Mock, and daughter-in-law, Marisa Grimes, thank you for joining our family and becoming a part of what makes us strong.

To my grandchildren, Hudson, Grace, and Lane Mock and Atlas Grimes, you are our joy, entertainment, and so much more. I am gifted to know you, our precious gifts from God.

Special thanks to the Baylor Bears and Tampa Bay Buccaneers for seeing my potential and inviting me to join your teams. You honed my discipline by pushing me to my limits and elevating my play both on and off the field. Because of you, I now have two extended families: one in my native Texas and another in my adopted state of Florida.

I couldn't have written this book without my ghostwriters, Scott and Jocelyn Carbonara, and their team of publishing and design specialists from Spiritus Communications (Amy Weinstein, Chip Thrasher, and Phil Studdard). Scott and Jocelyn interviewed my wife and me for days, pulling this story out of us while providing some needed therapy along the way! As I read through this book, I swear they got inside my head as they put my story to paper. Thank you. You are now family.

Thank you to Jenny Lisk of Bluhen Books for your impeccable project management of my book launch. Your passion and expertise were crucial to turning this book into a touchdown!

Thank you to Lisa Vetter of Tour de Force Speakers for your ongoing drive to find me the right speaking audiences—and for all the extra support in sharing my message with those who most need it. Your personal dedication to my mission means the world.

Finally, I thank my heavenly Father for not giving up on me. The Lord protected me from myself and my addiction, giving me this extra life, and restoring my family. I've learned the meaning of Jeremiah 29:11-13 (NIV):

> *For I know the plans I have for you, declares the Lord, plans to prosper you and not to harm you, plans to give you hope and a future. Then you will call on me and come and pray to me, and I will listen to you. You will seek me and find me when you seek me with all your heart.*

Just as God extended His ever-present love, forgiveness, and healing in my struggles, I am honored to be used by God to give back to others who still struggle.

Randy Grimes

Special Resource for the Reader: A Personal Note from Randy Grimes for Military Veterans, First Responders, Professional Athletes, and More

As an interventionist who has personally struggled with addiction, few things are more crucial to me than having an on-call treatment center that I know and trust. If you or a loved one struggles with a substance use disorder, you also know how challenging it is to navigate treatment options when they're most needed.

That's why I confidently refer people who need help to **WhiteSands Treatment Center**—a nationally-recognized inpatient and outpatient behavioral health and addiction treatment provider.

As one of the largest private insurance treatment centers in America, WhiteSands was founded with the overarching philosophy that it **was time to raise industry standards for the quality of treatment, comfort of patients, and long-term sobriety rates.**

Today, WhiteSands celebrates being named the #1 addiction treatment center in Florida for two years in a row by *Newsweek* **(2021).** They operate three inpatient and eighteen outpatient centers located throughout central and southwest Florida—accepting patients from across the country.

Levels of Care

At WhiteSands, all services share common elements in providing comprehensive, individualized care for co-occurring disorders. They employ MD, PhD, and nursing level staff skilled in the diagnosis of psychopathology, who are cross-trained in addictions and substance-related disorders. Services include:

- Inpatient Detox (Medically Assisted Detox)
- Residential/Intensive Inpatient Treatment
- Day-Night Treatment (transition from inpatient to outpatient environment with housing)
- Intensive Outpatient Treatment With Residence (IOP—further transitioning)

Life Skills

The overall philosophy of the Life Skills Program assists each patient not only in developing the skills to maintain long-term sobriety, but also in engaging in their most successful, happy, and balanced life.

Wellness Program

WhiteSands created a Recovery and Wellness Program to address concerns over the transition between leaving inpatient treatment and entering the next phase of recovery.

Why WhiteSands?

The company's founders recognized that national relapse rates were abysmal, and treatment protocols had remained stagnant for many years. Founded in 2014, WhiteSands treats around 2,000 patients annually. Today, they aim to ensure their treatment program stands well above their competitors, treating patients as individuals—while also providing many comforts of a home environment.

WhiteSands is a member of the National Association of Addiction Treatment Providers, accredited by the Joint Commission, a Veteran's Choice addiction treatment provider, and has received LegitScript's Addiction Treatment Certification for each of its facilities. With a renowned clinical team,

WhiteSands' leaders are constantly innovating to raise the bar for the utmost in quality, individualized care.

If you or a loved one needs help, I personally recommend that you reach out today to WhiteSands Treatment Center's highly-trained admissions staff.

Visit WStreatment.com or call (813) 296-8177.

ABOUT THE AUTHOR

A former NFL center whose successful career spanned ten years with the Tampa Bay Buccaneers, Randy Grimes used prescription pills to treat his career-related injuries. Those pills fed an addiction that would last more than twenty years.

Upon retiring from the NFL, Randy fell deeper into his addiction—eventually jeopardizing his family and everything he held dear. "In football, I always had a playbook—and a team—to give me my next move, and support me in the game," states Randy. "Without that structure, I didn't know what to do; I lost myself, as my addiction took over."

After losing a former teammate to an overdose, Randy finally had the courage to raise his hand and accept help. "I literally crawled into treatment," states Randy. "And the tools I found there saved my life. I prayed that God would open the gates of heaven and let me in. Instead, He opened the gates of hell and let me out!"

A strong advocate for recovery, Randy launched Pro Athletes in Recovery to help athletes find addiction treatment and recovery resources. Randy has worked closely with the NFL Player Care Foundation, After the Impact Fund, Gridiron Greats, and the Baseball Assistance Team to bring further awareness and treatment services to professional athletes and their families. As a result, hundreds of former professional athletes have since been treated. Randy was recognized in 2018 as a National Goodwill Ambassador. In 2019, Randy was inducted into the Gridiron Greats Hall of Fame, and he also received the Baylor Football Legend Award.

Randy's passion does not end with athletes; Randy believes that "when families get well, addicts get well." Randy has performed countless interventions across the US and in five countries—bringing hope and healing when all seems lost.

As of May of 2021, Randy and Lydia have been married for thirty-nine years, and they work together with family interventions. Randy is regularly a keynoter for corporate events and conferences—and contributor on national TV networks and media including *The New York Times*, NFL Network, ESPN, *Anderson Cooper 360°*, *Father Albert*, CNN, Fox Sports, MSNBC, Fox News, SiriusXM Sports, and countless others.

To connect with Randy, visit RandyGrimesSpeaks.com or ProAthletesInRecovery.org.

Made in the USA
Las Vegas, NV
09 March 2022